Paul Talafo

The Windows of Heaven to the heirs of God and Joint-heirs with Christ On the earth at this time

Paul Talafo

The Windows of Heaven to the heirs of God and Joint-heirs with Christ On the earth at this time

"Let the world see your good works and glorify your Father who is in heaven."

"Test Me now with this, says Jehovah of hosts, to see if I will not open the windows of heaven for you"

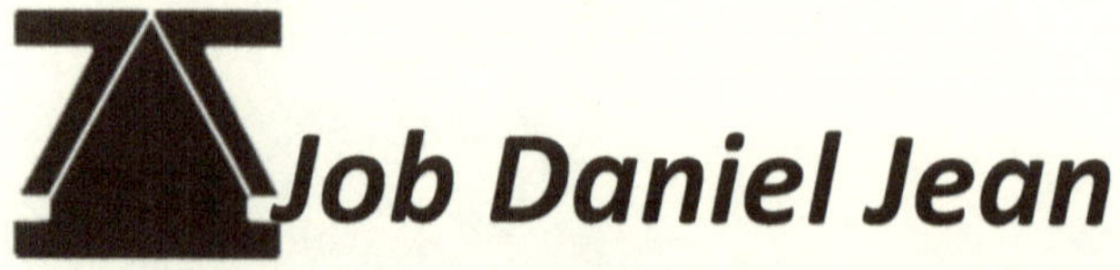

Unless otherwise indicated, all Scripture quotations are from the electronic Modern King James Version (eMKJV).

The Windows of Heaven to the heirs of God and joint-heirs with Christ on the earth at this time

Paul Talafo, 2019

ISBN: 979-10-94949-12-2
Printed in the United States of America
Copyright © 2019 by Paul Talafo

Job Daniel Jean
Ministère chrétien pour l'enseignement
job.daniel.jean@gmail.com

This book is an English translation of the French book *Les écluses des cieux aux héritiers de Dieu et cohéritiers avec Christ sur la terre en ce temps-ci*

Table of contents

Introduction

A person who discovers that he is a beneficiary of a wealthy man's inheritance seeks his fortune to recover it. The guardian of the inheritance then makes a point of honor to reveal to the heir the totality of the death capital available, and all the conditions required to get it. Finally the heir will meet the said conditions as quickly as possible in order to take his due. Believe me, even after he has perceived his inheritance, the heir will still have time to read and re-read the testament, just to make sure that nothing has been forgotten. Why? Because he wants to **have all of his share with him**. Needless to say that, if the guardian of the testament is at the other end of the world, the heir will move heaven and earth to reach him.

These are the habits of the men and women of this world. Can we imagine the Almighty God leaving an inheritance to negligent heirs? Negative. However, via the attitude of nowadays Christians, we must recognize that no inheritance has been so overlooked as the Old and New Testaments of God.

God left to men and women a book summarizing His deeds, from Genesis to Revelation, a book called "Old and New

Testaments" – Tanakh for Jews. This is the book of God for His heirs who are also referred to as *joint-heirs with Christ*. Scripture affirms the following:

> *«And if we are children, then we are heirs;* ***heirs of God and joint-heirs with Christ;*** *so that if we suffer with Him, we may also be glorified together»* (**Romans 8:17**).

The Apostle Paul foretold about two thousand years ago the events of the end times with these words:

> *«For a time will be when they will not endure sound doctrine, but they will heap up teachers to themselves according to their own lusts, tickling the ear.* ***And they will turn away their ears from the truth and will be turned to myths»*** (**2 Timothy 4:3-4**).

What is the part of Scripture in the living of Christians today? Very little and poor. Not that Christians do not read them, but they do not make them their main focal point. They prefer to listen to the Sunday sermons and, from time to time, take a sneak peek into the Scriptures, just to have a good conscience before God. Yet they have before them the Testament of God for His heirs, joint-heirs with Christ. We cannot say so much about tv-shows and internet. These two activities captivate the attention of Christians as much as the pagans of the world.

How can one imagine that an heir does not read in depth the God's Testament that assures him more wealth than any human or earthly institution can pass on? Must we understand that the heirs of God, joint-heirs with Christ, are not interested in this inheritance?

Let us remember that in many parables, Jesus reproached His contemporaries with a casual attitude towards His Father, to the point of exclaiming:

> *«If you then, being evil, know how to give good gifts to your children, how much more **shall your Father in heaven give good things to those who ask Him?**»* (**Matthew 7:11**).

We can draw the following parallel:

> *«If you then, being evil, know how to <u>leave fortunes to your heirs</u>, how much more **shall your Father in heaven <u>leave best fortunes to His heirs and joint-heirs with Christ?</u>**»*.

This book is inspired by this lament that God addresses to His children as above, His heirs, joint-heirs with Christ. It explores the essence of the riches that God has left to Christians in His Son Jesus Christ. It is not necessary to wait for the return of Christ to take possession of it because they are ALREADY accessible as it is written:

> *«There is no man that has left house or brothers or sisters or father or mother or wife*

> *or children or lands for My (Jesus) sake and the Gospel's sake, but he shall receive a hundredfold **NOW IN THIS TIME**, houses and brothers and sisters and mothers and children and lands **with persecutions**, and in the world to come, eternal life»* (**Mark 10:29-30**).

To believe that the promises of the Gospel will only be accessible after the return of Christ is to deprive ourselves of tremendous blessings on the earth. Only Christians, active in the exploration of the Scriptures, are aware of it. They are appropriating the inheritance that God has left, ***NOW IN THIS TIME, no matter the persecutions***. They just have to explore the Testament of God, their Testament. The latter is worth more than all the assembled inheritances of the earth. The inheritance of men is transmitted from one generation to another until the end of time. The Testament of God gives its beneficiaries eternal inheritance: eternal life and the windows of heaven.

Unless otherwise notice, all Bible quotations are from the Modern King James Version (MKJV). They are pasted in this book for a reason. **Matthew 5:10-13** means *the book of Matthew, chapter 5, verses 10 to 13*. For the sake of truth, we were careful to mention each Bible verse with respect to the historical context, highlighting the essential part in **bold**. The reader may find boring the full reproduction of Bible verses rather than footnotes. This was done on purpose because memorized verses tend to suffer discrepancies as time passes. Is it due to memory failure or evil action? We presume a bit of both. Is this the reason why the

Israelites, after a long period of obedience, began to transgress the commandments of God? Possible. We note that Moses instructed the Israelites to *bind the commandments for a sign upon their hand, as frontlets between their eyes, and to write them upon the posts of their house, and on their gates* (**Deuteronomy 6:8-9**). This warning of Moses is not fortuitous. The reader is therefore invited not to be exasperated with the reproduction of the Scriptures, but rather to read them studiously. He will notice that some verses which he thought he had memorized well, come in a different way. We have put in boxes very important notices. Finally, all the pronouns referring to the Lord God have been put in capital letter, for the sake of both accuracy and God's holiness. May the Lord God accompany you reader, open your mind and intelligence to seize the length and depth of His love for the men and women He approves of, in addition to His call to the first resurrection. Indeed *"Blessed and holy is he who has part in the **first resurrection**. The second death has no authority over these, but they will be priests of God and of Christ, and will reign with Him a thousand years"* (**Revelation 20:6**).

Threat on the inheritance ignored by Christians

Honestly, if it were necessary to describe the abundant inheritance of God, all the books of the earth would not be enough because the inheritance of God is as great as God Himself. This chapter does not claim to be an exhaustive list of this inheritance. However, it will give a glimpse of it by exhorting the heirs of God, co-heirs with Christ, to do everything to possess this fortune. The ultimate goal is to denounce the indifference of Christians to an accessible divine inheritance, a legacy greater than all the fortunes of the earth.

Story of a traveler who did ignore his rights

A traveler boarded for a week-long boat trip. He had given his last money for the ticket. He therefore decided to travel famished, only taking sips of water every day. He could endure three days in this state, weakening inwardly, although he did everything to hide it from other travelers. As Christian, he did not see himself begging for his daily bread, which was to his credit. That's why he dressed in thick and warm clothes. The reality was, however, that it was difficult for him to endure this state of weakness. What was he going to do?

He came to guess that the cook of the boat could make him a meal as payment for some small works of the kind: blow of broom here, small cleaning by there. He gave himself some time to think about before making a move. Two days later, unable to bear it any more, he went to the cook. He was surprised when the cook said that he had been missing for five days among his guests. He was told that his traveler ticket comprised a meal on board. Indeed the cook had been noticed that a traveler was missing during meals. *'Can you confirm that I am entitled to a free meal on board?'* The traveler asked the cook again, stunned. *'Yes sir, please have a seat! What do you want to eat? Here is the menu of the day'*.

Our traveler, a Christian, came to realize how ignorant of his rights had almost ruined his health. His meal was there, near him, but he did not know it. He was like one who possessed nothing whereas he possessed an essential good: his daily bread guaranteed by the Lord according to the prayer taught to the disciples.

This is the situation of many Christians today. They do not know that they have things. They are like those victims who, in distress, are unaware of the advantages granted by their subscribed insurance.

Ignorance, the most devastating illness of all time

> *«My people are destroyed for lack of knowledge»* **Hosea 4:6**.

Ignorance can have many faces. I will mention a few. Being misdiagnosed by a doctor and receiving inappropriate drugs. Undertake a job one is not skilled for. Take a dead end road; if we had known it, we would have taken no risk. Buy a defective property. Vote for the wrong candidate. Take fake shortcuts. Contract a bad marriage. Trust the bad bookmaker. Choose the wrong color. Being in the wrong place at the wrong time. Missing the legacy of an unknown distant ascendant.

The tragedy, in terms of ignorance, is that this disease does not appear in any Public Health program. The only remedy against ignorance is knowledge, provided it is desired. Can we know why, with equal talent, an athlete succeeds better than another? Why does a musician live decently while another faces hardship? Why, with equal income, an employee succeeds more than another?

It's all about choice and opportunity. Ignorance is the essential factor behind a failure. One answers 'yes' and another 'no' to the same question, an everything changes. The unfortunate one will be filled with regret his lifelong wondering what would have happened if he has answered otherwise.

The Lord affirms that *His people are destroyed for lack of knowledge.* Christians are not immune to the serious consequences of ignorance. In the end, knowledge is a light illuminating the road of Christians, preventing them from mistakes.

Let's not forget that the mother wants her child to acquire solid rudiments to face adversity and hardship. She knows that the more educated her child is, the more immune he will be against adversity. God has the same concern for His children, the Christians. God knows that the more His child knows» about Him, the better he will be protected against the traps of the enemy – Satan – *who comes only to steal and destroy.*

The opposite of ignorance is knowledge. The final aim of knowledge is wisdom. Ignorance thus reveals a lack of wisdom. It is the lack of wisdom which explains the mistake of the brilliant star, alias Satan, who wanted to reach the Throne of Almighty God thanks to his appearance and splendor. If Satan were wise, he should have glorified the Almighty God, the Author of his appearance and splendor, rather than standing against Him by means of these same assets. The Scripture affirms moreover:

> «*So that, **by means of the Church, the manifold wisdom of God might become known to the principalities and powers that are in heaven** (Satan included): which wisdom he arranged ages before, and he hath executed it by Jesus the Messiah our Lord*» (**Ephesians 3:10-11/ Bible Murdoch**).

If the principalities and powers **in heaven** (Satan included) **now** know the wisdom of God, then we can conclude that this wisdom was lacking before. And now, through the Church, this wisdom is accessible to them in many ways. This explains why ignorance is not only the disease of humans. Celestial beings are also affected. This confirms that ignorance is the most devastating disease of all times and ages.

Knowledge as a cure for ignorance and poverty

> *«And this is life eternal, **that they might know You,** the only true God, and Jesus Christ whom You have sent»* **John 17:3**.

> *«Then we shall know, if we follow on to know Jehovah»* **Hosea 6:3**.

Conscious of the danger of ignorance in the life of His creatures, God prescribes them knowledge. Knowledge is God's answer to ignorance. Alas many creatures think that money is the best answer to the needs of life. They argue that *money means happiness*. God has another opinion. Knowledge is the answer His creatures need to triumph. You can have all the gold of the world and succumb to an ugly disease, a sudden illness like mere mortals.

In fact, if a man could dig deeply, or if he were more lucid, he would see that God is right in saying that *knowledge is worth more than refined gold*. What makes the superiority of one nation over another? It is its ability to create, invent, innovate and distribute; activities that earn money and support growth. People that do not innovate are imposed the culture and way of life of innovative people. History of men is rich of such examples.

In these times of the end, with the United States of America as the dominating country worldwide, we can see that its innovations say Internet, smartphones, tablets, movies and TV series, have invaded the world and created new habits. It is thanks to its abilities at innovating that the United States has acquired the financial and military power that we know today. Money is always the consequence of innovation and production. Knowledge therefore produces wealth and power.

Scripture goes the same path. Here are some examples:

> «*Wisdom is the main thing;* **Get wisdom; and with all your getting** *get understanding*» **(Proverbs 4:7)**.

> «*Receive my* **instruction and not silver; and knowledge rather than choice gold**. *For* **wisdom is better than rubies;** *and all the things that may be desired are not to be compared to it*» **(Proverbs 8:10-11)**.

It is with knowledge that we make good decisions for the future. The life of each of us is often summed up in all decisions we had made before, good or bad. You are either at the top, at the bottom, or in the middle of the social class. It's the result of decisions made in your life, with the knowledge in the background.

Knowledge acquired in quantity and quality influences the existence of all creatures of God: men and celestial beings (angels) without exception.

The devil likes to mislead man into ephemeral riches, far from true knowledge which is God

The scriptures help to understand why the devil encourages men to devote all their strength to money at the expense of knowledge. This is because at first, created as a shining star, the devil became passionate about trading and transactions of all kinds (**Ezekiel 28:16 and 18**). He is therefore a great master of trading. Second, it is because of the lack of wisdom that he perverted his ways ahead to coveting the Throne of God. Scripture says:

> *«So that, by means of the Church, the manifold wisdom of God might become known to the principalities and powers that are in heaven»* **(Ephesians 3:10/ Bible Murdoch)**.

This verse from Paul's epistle clearly shows that the principalities and powers in heavenly places – including the devil – needed to be evangelized, that is, to receive, through the Church, the greatly diversified wisdom of God. If the devil had had this wisdom at the beginning, he would not have ventured to covet the Throne of God relying on his appearance and splendor.

The devil does not want humans to discover his recurring faults, mainly his lack of wisdom. He likes to lock humans up in the unbridled search for material comfort at the expense of wisdom. Nevertheless, Scriptures regard the treasures of the earth as ephemeral objects. Jesus says indeed:

> «***Do not lay up treasures on the earth for yourselves, where moth and rust corrupt, and where thieves break through and steal****. But lay up treasures in heaven for yourselves, where neither moth nor rust corrupt, and where thieves do not break through nor steal. For where your treasure is, there will your heart be also*» (**Matthew 6:19-21**).

The facts attest perfectly that no earthly wealth is eternal. But because they are often slow to shift from one owner to another, we feel that wealth can last forever. There are indeed individual wealth that can worth centuries-equivalent-wages. So we hear that such a rich man has enough to feed a hundred generations of descendants. On paper, it seems true; but in reality, it is not. An European saying says: "*The father amasses, the son manages and the grandson destroys.*" This is another way of saying that it is hard for wealth to pass on until the third or fourth generation of men and women. Experience seems to attest to this truth. The harmful effects of theft are known. Many people have been ruined by thieves. In the verse **Matthew 6:19-21** above, the moth symbolizes bad weather such as floods and storms. If you travel over the planet, you will notice many buildings abandoned because of floods, hurricanes, lightning, etc. Their owners did not have time or money to restore them. Rust, on the other hand, represents the depreciation and aging of goods. Sooner or later, in fact, we will have to renovate a property if we do not want to see its value going down indefinitely.

What became of Solomon's great achievements and all the gold he received each year? Where are the Egyptian pyramids now? Where are the magnificent works of the powerful kingdoms of antiquity – Babylon, Greece, Persia and Rome? These riches are today plundered or fossilized under hundreds of meters of land and in the abyss of the oceans. Yet, their owners have predicted their everlasting prevalence.

It is therefore obvious that no earthly wealth is eternal, yet man thinks the opposite. It is certainly the fault of the devil who has obscured his intelligence behind sophisticated calculations. The devil knows full well that no wealth is eternal, but that he hides it from humans blinded by greed. Only the knowledge of God is an eternal wealth. But the devil wants to divert man from this truth. The devil was the victim of his own ignorance, lack of knowledge and wisdom. He does not want man to access knowledge because man will escape his tricks.

The riches amassed in heaven, as counseled by the Lord in **Matthew 6:19-21** above, are based on the commandments of God and sanctification. The devil advises to struggle to acquire ephemeral wealth – buildings, cars, financial comfort, etc. – while the Lord advises to obey Him in all circumstances to acquire, in return, eternal riches, inaccessible to various thieves and destroyers. Jesus Christ says indeed:

> «***Seek first*** *the kingdom of God and His righteousness; and all these things (wealth) shall be added to you*» (**Matthew 6:33**).

First inheritance: the gift of the Holy Spirit, the Spirit of truth, the Comforter

«*When the **Comforter** has come, whom I will send to you from the Father, the **Spirit of truth** who proceeds from the Father, He shall testify of Me*» **John 15:26**.

«*Peter said to them, repent and be baptized, every one of you, in the name of Jesus Christ to remission of sins, and **you shall receive the gift of the Holy Spirit***» **Acts 2:38**.

Identity of Christians: Christians are saints, members of the kingdom of heaven

The true identity of the Christian is revealed through the blessings that God gives to him. He who receives the gift of prophecy is a prophet. He who receives the gift of shepherd is a pastor. Whoever receives the gift of teaching is a teacher. Just as an evangelist is the one who receives the gift of preaching. **He who**

receives the Holy Spirit is a saint, a member of the kingdom of heaven.

Jesus made it clear that His kingdom was not of this world. He says to the unbelieving Jews:

> «*You are from beneath; **I am from above**. You are of this world; **I am not of this world***» (**John 8:23**).

Jesus indicated that His presence on the earth also meant that His kingdom had come down to earth:

> «*But if I cast out demons by the Spirit of God, **then the kingdom of God has come to you***» (**Matthew 12:28**).

Later, in His last prayer to Father, Jesus declares that His disciples, called to pursue His mission after Him, were not of this world too, though called to live in the world. He said indeed:

> «*I have given them Your word, and the world has hated them **because they are not of the world**, even as I am not of the world. I do not pray for You to take them out of the world, but for You to keep them from the evil. **They are not of the world**, even as I am not of the world*» (**John 17:14-16**).

Christians are no longer of the world because they now belong to a different kingdom, that of Christ: the kingdom of heaven. Christians are therefore saints. Scripture gives them this qualifier abundantly in the epistles of the apostles. Here are a few:

> *«For it has pleased those of Macedonia and Achaia to make a certain contribution **for the poor saints in Jerusalem***» (**Romans 15:26**).

> *«Paul, an apostle of Jesus Christ by the will of God, **to the saints who are in Ephesus, and faithful in Christ Jesus**. Grace be to you, and peace from God our Father and from the Lord Jesus Christ»* (**Ephesians 1:1-2**).

In the acts and epistles of the apostles, the words 'saint' and 'Christian' are equal. The word 'saint' is even used extensively because, in the first century of Christian era, the word 'Christian' was as pejorative as the word 'sect' today.

From the status of saint, member of the kingdom of heaven, everything changes for the Christian, as we shall see below.

The natural man inherits from his father: spirit, soul and body

> «*May the God of peace Himself sanctify you, and may **your whole spirit and soul and body** be preserved blamelessly at the coming of our Lord Jesus Christ*» **1 Thessalonians 5:23**.

According to Scripture, man is made up of a spirit, a soul and a body through which human nature is defined. From one generation to another, humans transmit to their descendants what they naturally possess: a body, a spirit and a soul. Since humans cannot give birth to wild animals, reptiles, fish and birds, but only to humans, we are certain that future generations will have a body, a spirit and a soul like Adam and Eve. That's why only humans inherit humans. Never has an angel inherited a human. Never has a lion, a raven or a bird naturally inherited the man.

By making the Christian His heir and joint-heir with Christ, God gives Christian the divine nature. We will further explain God's invitation to move from human nature to the divine nature.

We must take note that humans inherit humans. This is the main base of the natural heritage. To inherit the nature of man, one must be like him. One must have been begotten by him. Whoever has not been engendered by Gerome, naturally cannot inherit Gerome. If then God sees Christians as His heirs and joint-heirs with Christ, it is because **God recognizes that He has engendered them in Christ**. This is what Scripture attests:

> *«For we are His workmanship, **created in Christ Jesus** to good works, which God has before ordained that we should walk in them»* **(Ephesians 2:10)**.

> *«But as many as received Him, **He gave to them authority to become the children of God**, to those who believe on His name, **who were born**, not of bloods, nor of the will of the flesh, nor of the will of man, but were born **of God**»* **(John 1:12-13)**.

God says that the Christian is begotten by Him, just as men and women are begotten by their parents. **Being born of God grants divine attributes as much as being born of biological parents grants human attributes**. The Christian must not ignore this truth. He is even invited to claim it because he has received the faith for it. It is sad that Christians do not take themselves as sons whom God has begotten as much as they are aware of having biological fathers. God wants Christians to take Him seriously since the affirmation is of Him.

But the Christian inherits the Spirit of God and the divine nature

Just as a newborn baby inherits the human spirit at birth, because his parents possess a human spirit, the Christian inherits the Holy Spirit when he confesses and believes that Jesus Christ is the Expiatory Lamb offered as a ransom for humanity's sin. From the regeneration of his spirit (new birth), the Christian inherits the Holy Spirit. Jesus says to the Pharisee Nicodemus:

> *«Unless a man is born of water and the Spirit, he cannot enter into the kingdom of God»* (**John 3:5**).

The new birth or Christendom is a matter of the Holy Spirit. Scripture affirms that *if anyone has not the Spirit of Christ, he is none of His* (**Romans 8:9**). The new birth has nothing to do with the activities carried out in the churches. Some churches even entrusted pagans with activities for the building of the body of Christ. None of these activities will give these pagans the status of Christian. For it is by being born of the Spirit that one becomes a Christian, according to the words of Jesus; and nothing else.

Hence we should not confuse on the real identity of the Christian. The Christian has the Holy Spirit in him, the Spirit of Christ, the Spirit of God, the Spirit of truth, the Comforter.

As discussed above, if God has established that the Christian is His heir and joint-heir with Christ, then the Christian inherits the nature of God, a divine nature.

The requirements of the divine nature inherited by the Christian

«Through which (glory and virtue) He has given to us exceedingly great and precious promises, so that by these you might be **partakers of the divine nature***, having escaped the corruption that is in the world through lust»* **2 Peter 1:4**.

«But you (Christians) have not so learned Christ, if indeed you have heard Him and were taught by Him, as the truth is in Jesus. For you ought to **put off the old man** *(according to your way of living before) who is corrupt according to the deceitful lusts, and* **be renewed in the Spirit of your mind***. And you should* **put on the new man, who according to God was created in righteousness and true holiness»** **Ephesians 4:20-24**.

«Therefore **put to death your members which are on the earth***: fornication, uncleanness, passion, evil desire, and covetousness which is*

> *idolatry. (...) Do not lie to one another,* **having put off the old man** *with his deeds and* **having put on the new**, *having been renewed in knowledge according to the image of Him who created him»* **Colossians 3:5,9-10**.

In ascending these Scriptures from below upward, we learn that the Christian is summoned to *put off the old man* – corrupted by the passions and lusts that were wrought there – in order to take on the new nature whose characteristic is that it is renewed according to the image of the God who created it. **Ephesians 4:24** states that it is God who created the new nature *in righteousness and true holiness*. **Verse 23** indicates that the new nature is received thanks to the *Spirit that renews the mind (intelligence)* of the Christian. Thus, we see that the presence of the Holy Spirit in the Christian aims, among other things, to establish the **holiness of God in his mind** in order to change his tendencies, and to make him pass from old human tendencies to the divine tendencies which will grow to know God in truth – through His acts of justice.

Therefore the Christian must not prevent the renewal of his intelligence by the Holy Spirit in order to modify his nature entirely. In fact, it is not a question of improving the old human nature because human is incapable of correction. It is a question of getting rid of the human nature in favor of the new divine nature inoculated by the Holy Spirit. For before the Holy Spirit came to dwell in the spirit of the Christian, the latter was ruled by his unregenerate natural spirit. At regeneration, the Holy Spirit settles in the spirit of the Christian – *Your body is a temple of the Holy Spirit in you, whom you have of God* (**1 Corinthians 6:19**).

The Christian must not be ashamed of this renewed nature – divine – even if such an affirmation may seem surrealistic in this world. The Christian being **born of water and Spirit**, it is obvious that he will be animated by a nature other than earthly. It is a life-giving nature as it is written:

> *«If the Spirit of the One who raised up Jesus from the dead dwells in you, the One who raised up Christ from the dead **shall also make your mortal bodies alive by His Spirit who dwells in you***» (**Romans 8:11**).

Other translation:

> *«If the Spirit of Him, who raised our Lord Jesus Messiah from the dead, dwelleth in you; He who raised our Lord Jesus Messiah from the dead, **will also vivify your dead bodies, because of His spirit that dwelleth in you***» (**Romans 8:11/Bible Murdoch 1851**).

It is this life inoculated into the Christian that is of divine nature. Our bodies are mortal, but the life that is inoculated by the Holy Spirit is divine. It is this nature that is being renewed day by day in order to bring the Christian to the stature of Christ (**Ephesians 4:13**). We make it clear that the Holy Spirit resides in the spirit of the Christian at regeneration. It is from that human spirit that the Holy Spirit introduces the divine life into the intelligence (mind), the feelings and the will of the Christian. It is said then that this Christian has a renewed intelligence, renewed sentiments and renewed will to the glory of God the Father. This Christian therefore passes from the human nature to the divine nature although his body remains mortal.

How does the Christian move from human nature to the divine nature?

*«But you (Christians) have not so learned Christ, if indeed you have heard Him and were taught by Him, as the truth is in Jesus. For you ought to **put off the old man** (according to your way of living before) who is corrupt according to the deceitful lusts, and **be renewed in the Spirit of your mind**. And you should put on the new man, who according to God was created in righteousness and true holiness»* **Ephesians 4:20-24.**

It is evident from **Ephesians 4:20-24** that the transition from human nature to the divine nature involves a **stripping** and a **renewal**. These two actions are made possible by the presence of the Holy Spirit in the Christian. Without the Spirit of Christ, it is useless to try because it is impossible for the natural man.

If the Christian does not put a heart to it, in this process of **stripping** and **renewal**, he will soon realize that his life is no different from life before conversion. The presence of the Holy Spirit regenerates the Christian who passes from death (natural man) to life (spiritual man).

The Lord invites the Christian to the **stripping away** of the old human nature and to the **renewal** in an incorruptible divine nature because His Spirit dwells in the Christian. Whatever the difficulties, the Christian must trust Christ, and what he desires will come true. This is the principle of faith in Christ: *the **substance** of things hoped for, the **evidence** of things not seen* (**Hebrews 11:1**). One must first hope for what is unseen, while having the heart – the inner eyes – fixed on Christ. It is then that God will bring forth the unseen to the visible world; so the **evidence** is complete.

Once aware of the necessity of putting off the old human nature for the benefit of the new divine nature, the Christian must accept the choices of God in all circumstances of his life. Among the tendencies that must be put off, **Colossians 3:5** mentions in particular *misconduct, impurity, passions, bad desires and greed.*

There are a plethora of other tendencies that must be stripped away and that have a close or distant connection with them.

We must specify that putting off the old nature is not always easy. It is even a dry loss because, among old tendencies to put off, there are things with an appearance of virtue such as: *do not taste, do not eat, wait for a particular day, not in such a place, etc.* Some trends are even praised by local laws.

So the Christian should avoid building his life on public opinion and traditions of this world. Only the word of God should illuminate his way. What is forbidden by the word of God, he will have to avoid it such as, in our day, homosexuality which alas is gradually tolerated in the world (**1 Corinthians 6:10, 1 Timothy 1:10, Jude 1:7**). What the word of God allows, he must accept it, no matter the hostility of the world around, because *heaven and earth will pass but the word of God will not pass*. In fact all that is visible will pass. And the wise observer can already realize that Scriptures have remained unchanged while the countries have undergone many upheavals. The great countries of today – the United States of America, France, England, Russia, Brazil, India, China, Japan – were almost unknown in antiquity where Egypt, Greece, Italy (ancient Rome), Iran (ancient Persia) held the leading roles. It will be the same in the future because it is not certain that the advanced countries of today will still be at the forefront tomorrow. It may seem crazy to say that today, as it was crazy to imagine the fall of Egyptian pharaohs and Roman emperors whose rule lasted for centuries. But what has not changed and will never change is the word of God, *the sword of the Spirit*. The Word of God has withstood earthquakes, floods, wars, cultural, civilizational, social and political upheavals, as well as weather and catastrophes of all kinds. Sometimes the Word of God was not available, but always, it was found unchanged, immutable.

There is a strong tendency for Christians to imitate what is good in the world. We do not think that the acts of this world are all bad. However, while living in the world, Christians must make sure that their actions conform to the commandments of God. **What His word accepts, they must accept it. What His word rejects, they must reject it**. It is then that they will be the Christians God is proud of.

For example, the Lord asks not to take revenge, to leave Him the exclusivity of revenge. He asks Christians to be happy when one spread bad news about them because of Him. This warns Christians against any search for popular recognition. Those who wish to be praised in the world and those who are afraid of being looked down, cannot be the Christians that Jesus Christ seeks. The Lord asks the Christians to turn the second cheek after being slapped, to walk one more miles after being forced to make one, to give a second tunic after being deprived of the first. This is possible only if one possesses the Holy Spirit in oneself. And Christians must not find excuses and pretexts to avoid it. Likewise, the Lord will ask them to love their enemies and to greet them. They must obey to be His disciples. That is how they will strip themselves of the old human nature in favor of the new, divine, incorruptible one.

May the Christian ask and make sure that the Holy Spirit dwells in him

> «*But if anyone has not the Spirit of Christ, he is none of His*» **Romans 8:9**.

Make no mistake, he who does not have the Holy Spirit, the Spirit of Christ, does not belong to Him. The good news for every Christian is that the Holy Spirit has been freely promised to those who ask for It: "*God does not give the Spirit by measure*" (**John 3:34**). The Christian must therefore make sure that he has the Holy Spirit dwelling in him. The work of the Holy Spirit in the Christian is real and detectable by him. The Christian must have no doubt about the presence and work of the Holy Spirit in him. If in doubt, he must ask the Lord for confirmation, but secretly – as explained later. The Lord will not be offended by his request.

The reality is that there are people who, calling themselves Christians, do not have the Holy Spirit in them (**Acts 19:2-6**). It is difficult to identify such Christians because Scripture states that only Jesus Christ knows those who belong to Him (**2 Timothy 2:19**). Any other teaching is inappropriate. The Lord has not entrusted anyone to check on who has the Holy Spirit and who doesn't. If such a checking were to be put in place, this drift would lead the Church to confusion. The devil could use it to destroy many true Christians, portraying them as pagans whereas they are saints. If the Pharisees have said of Jesus that He was of Satan (**Matthew 12:24**), will the faithful of the devil – disguised as angels of light in the churches – not defame true Christians to sow confusion? According to **Acts 19:2-6** above, Apostle Paul acts with caution in asking his listeners whether *they received the Holy Spirit when they believed*. He never deliberately declared that these people did not have the Holy Spirit in them. It was after a real investigation, helped by the same people, that he came to the conclusion that they had not received the Holy Spirit. Then he solved the problem immediately.

Precision. When Apostle John asks *to test the spirits to know if they are of God* (**1 John 4:1**), he invites to be wary of those who make unfounded or erroneous remarks, while pretending to be Christians, in the only purpose of fooling the sheep of the Lord. Wolves disguised as sheep have several times looted the sheepfold of the Lord in the history of the Church from the first century to the present day. A certain vigilance could have avoided many of these dramas. For example, at the time of John's warning, some argued that Christ never came in the flesh. This is why, following the verse calling for vigilance, Apostle John declares:

> *«By this you know the Spirit of God: every spirit that confesses that **Jesus Christ has come in the flesh** is of God; and every spirit that does not confess that Jesus Christ has come in the flesh is not of God. And this is the antichrist you heard is coming, and even now is already in the world»* (**1 John 4:2-3**).

By this warning, Apostle John prevented the adepts of this false doctrine from spreading it in the Church. It can be said that the apostle's warning bore fruit because very few people profess this heresy today.

Once again, it is in the interest of the Christian to ensure that he has the Holy Spirit, the Spirit of truth, the Spirit of Christ within him. Having the Holy Spirit in oneself is the beginning of a prosperous Christian life. Otherwise, this person deceives himself. That he does not say to himself that his participation in Church's activities will give him the epithet of a Christian in front of the Lord. We are Christians in front of the Lord and not in front of men and women attending a church. We do not flatter the Lord. We do not buy it with the activities – sacrifices. If a Christian, in doubt, puts the question to the Lord, the Lord will enlighten him because He loves the truth. Without the Holy Spirit, no man has any inheritance in the kingdom of heaven. Any matter of verification of the presence of the Holy Spirit in oneself must be SECRET. We insist on the SECRET. The Christian must not reveal his doubt to anyone, to other Christians of the Church, or even to pastors because he does not know who is really who. Let him bring this question secretly before the Lord, and God who sees in secret will enlighten him. The Christian will have no doubt about the Lord's response. The Lord will watch over it. A quick check is to ask the Lord to reveal how He sees us. He will give an image of our self as He sees it. I have known Christians who have gone through this process. Believe me, the results were uplifting. Above all, do not panic if the answer seems negative. It is not uncommon for doubts to spray into the life of a Christian. The prophet John the Baptist had doubts. Even if his example is not flattering, it indicates that at some point, doubt may appear. Apostle Paul also had doubts (**2 Corinthians 1:8-9**). Do not panic, the Lord will answer. He answered John the Baptist. He answered Paul (**v9**). He will answer also those who have doubts. It is better to start on the right foot, because we will not regret it. If ever the Christian realizes that he does not have the Holy Spirit, first he praises the Lord for revealing his true spiritual state. Repent before the Lord – even publicly if the sin in which he is entangled deserves repentance before men and women. May he sincerely ask God the Holy Spirit and he will see God respond to him with success. The Lord knows right now that he is dealing with a definitively repentant sinner. May he ask without hesitation, because Christ sincerely desires to give his Spirit to the men and women he approves. The Lord will never compromise on this issue. He will give His Spirit to anyone who sincerely asks Him – *how much more will the heavenly Father **give the Holy Spirit to those who ask Him*** (**Luke 11:13**). The purpose of this warning is not to scare anyone, but to build on a solid foundation for the good of the Christian.

God uses the familiar words of the world to talk to men

One of man's greatest dilemmas lies in his interpretation of God's commandments. Man has a hard time interpreting the words of the invisible God as he would of a person he sees. It is as if the invisibility of God makes Him non-existent and inactive among men. Wrong.

This is a real problem among humans. Man has trouble imagining a God accessible to the concerns of humans. We know how to approach a human being: just speak the same language as him and read well his body language. In any case, men and women of this world have always been able to communicate despite cultural, national and racial differences.

But God also communicates with men. Do not believe that the invisible God can only communicate through the languages of angels. Salvation in Christ, as Scripture reminds us, does not come from man, it is a gift from God (**Ephesians 2:8**). If God wants to save man, He will necessarily use a language accessible to man. This is what Jesus Christ did during His earthly journey: He used the sayings and scenes of everyday life to carry on His Father's message.

Man's discrimination against the invisible God, unlike the visible man, led Jesus to complain out loud:

> *«If you then, being evil, know how to give good gifts to your children, **how much more shall your Father in heaven give good things to those who ask Him?**»* (**Matthew 7:11**).

Jesus did not hesitate to denounce the hypocrisy of men: sincere towards their fellows, but false to God. Jesus asked for equal treatment. Christians do not seem to seriously take into account the words of the invisible God whereas He is real and active. Apostle Paul told his contemporaries that they must believe that God listens to their prayers for them to persevere in piety: "*He who comes to God **must believe that He is and that He is a rewarder** of those who diligently seek Him.*" (**Hebrews 11:6**). But to approach God, according to Scripture, is to enter a secret place where one does not see God. Nevertheless, although invisible, this God is present in the secret place. It is to this God that the Christian addresses himself and he must never doubt nor stop the practice.

Man's reflexes come partly from the fact that he was created in the image of God

As God created man in His image, the reflexes of man derive their sources, for a large part, from God. God also has certain known reflexes in the man He has created. Man must not believe that he comes from nothingness. He was created in the image of God. If man desires strongly to give the blow to an enemy, it is because this feeling comes from God who, by Moses, instituted the Law of retaliation: *tooth for tooth, eye for eye.*

In His wrath against Myriam's rebellion against Moses, God made this astonishing remark: "***If her father had but spit in her face, should she not be ashamed seven days?*** *Let her be shut out from the camp seven days, and after that let her be received*"(**Numbers 12:14**). This divine punishment is reported after Moses incited God to give up His anger against Myriam, who acted ignorantly. In his response, God was inspired by what would have happened if Myriam's father had spat in her face angrily: she would have been in confusion for seven days. God applied this human tradition to Myriam. Why? **Because God is close to the man He created in His image**.

In discovering how far man seems so distant and careless of Scripture, as if it were addressed to celestial beings and not men, it is understandable why many Christians read these Scriptures sparingly and casually. The religious man has always taken care to address the one he sees. That is why he loves to represent God by all kinds of effigies. By these means man is sure he is really speaking to God. In practice, even if he does not stand before an image of God, he likes to hold something in his hand that will remind him of God. Many animist African peoples swear by plunging their finger into the earth. Some put their hands on a visible object such as a tree. The Jews themselves stood either in front of the ark or in front of the Urim and the Toummim. It is by these visible means that men feel that God hears them.

The man has trouble talking alone in the secret. He needs to feel his listener by his senses. This is his biggest difficulty. So he regularly forgets that God is observing him because he takes the invisibility of God for God being absent. The man has trouble getting over to a listener whom he does not see. However invisible, God remains present and active.

God requires that the Christian walk by faith and not by sight. He forbids anyone to represent Him by any image or visible object. He is present, that's all. He demands that we believe in His existence when we stand in His presence in a secret place. To represent God by an effigy is to impose a place where God can be worshiped. God does not want man to impose such limitations. Jesus says to the Samaritan woman:

> «*The hour is coming when **you shall neither worship the Father in this mountain nor yet at Jerusalem**. (...) But the hour is coming, and now is, when **the true worshipers shall worship the Father in spirit and truth**, for the Father seeks such to worship Him. God is a spirit, and they who worship Him must worship in spirit and in truth*» (**John 4:21-24**).

Jesus says "*they who worship Him must...*" to indicate that one must approach an invisible God because the spirit is invisible. God being spirit, He REFUSES any representation of His person by a visible, palpable material object. HE DOES NOT WANT IT. His children would do better to comply.

Our Father, this wealthy Billionaire who is in heaven

We are accustomed to say of our Father that He is the Lord, the Highest, Almighty. It is not exaggerated to call Him Rich. Yes our Father the Richest because everything is from Him, by Him and for Him. Many will be surprised because we generally say those words to humans only. There are indeed billionaires among humans, individuals topping a great fortune. But God is also a Grand Billionaire in heaven since He is the One who creates all things. Having created all the precious stones (jewelries) for the eyes of men and women, the Creator of these stones, God, is a richest billionaire. Many Scripture quotations confirm this truth, no need to list them.

Hence the question: What billionaire has never worried about the future his heirs will reserve for his fortune? It is well-known that the kings of this world, topping great fortunes, have always been concerned about the ability of their heirs to preserve their inheritance after they depart. Thus, in many monarchies, there are special trainings for crown princes. The crown prince must necessarily follow courses that will ensure success after his ascending to the throne.

Billionaires of the world have the same concern. They are worried about the fate of their fortune after they depart, a fortune amassed during years of hardship. Many sons and daughters of high fortunes are usually sent to the most prestigious schools on the earth.

Do we think that the heavenly Father will not have the same concern for His heirs, joint-heirs with Christ? Christians must understand and keep in mind that their heavenly Father wants them to reach the perfect stature of Christ, to be able to assume the responsibilities that lie ahead. The Scriptures say:

> *«They (Christians) will be **priests of God and of Christ**, and will reign with Him a thousand years»* (**Revelation 20:6**).

To be *priest of God and of Christ*, and to *reign with Christ for a thousand years* are what awaits the Christian as soon as the Lord returns to earth. God takes this role very seriously. He will make sure that now, Christians give all to achieve this goal, his future mission.

The Christian must not neglect this future mission. The success of this mission requires thorough preparation during his living here on the earth. It is *sanctification without which no one will see the Lord*. Any negligence in this process of sanctification must be cast out.

So the Lord calls Christians to be vigilant: *Watch and pray ... Blessed is this servant whom the Master will find at work.* The Christian must not be mistaken about the related 'work'. The Lord affirms further: *He who loves Me keeps My commandments.* An exhortation recalled in the epistles of the apostles, from Apostle Paul to Apostle John. The 'work' we are talking about is: keeping the command of the Lord and sanctifying ourselves.

We always come back to the need to keep the Lord's commandments. To it, there is a lot to say. It is a pity that Christians are more attached to the visible activities of the Church than to the Word of God. The fault certainly to the tradition of the ancient Christians. Indeed, the Western world has Christianized faster than other continents such as Asia, Africa and America. Many Western Christians have experienced martyrdom because of their faith long before the Reform led by Martin Luther. Subsequently, many laws did consider Christianity as official religion. This formalism has laid the foundations for a tradition that nowadays Christians apply without discernment. And this is the nerve of the problem. Instead of revisiting the Scriptures to ensure that God's command is respected, nowadays Christians blindly apply the tradition of the elders. Jesus denounced this behavior among the Pharisees, saying:

> **«For laying aside the commandment of God, you hold the tradition of men, the dippings of pots and cups. And many other such things you do.** *And Jesus said to them,* **do you do well to set aside the commandment of God, so that you may keep your own tradition? (...) Making the word of God of no effect through**

your tradition which you have delivered»
(Mark 7:8-9, 13).

Like it or not, the implantation of Christianity in Europe was bloody with many compromises, most of which, if justified in the context of old time, are no longer justified today. Christians must revisit the Holy Scriptures and correct themselves under the guidance of the Holy Spirit, *the Comforter who will lead them into all truth.*

God resists caviar-Christians and low-cost Gospel

The caviar-Christian believes that everything is easy in the Lord Jesus Christ, easy and delicious like eating caviar. Wrong! These unstable Christians have received a low-cost gospel making great promises in the best of worlds. They were told that with God everything becomes easy. It is true that *the Lord's burden is light and His yoke is easy* (**Matthew 11:30**). However this is not a reason to believe that everything is gained by a click button.

Many Christians today spend hours in front of TV shows and internet streaming, viewing reality shows, navigating from one website to another by click buttons.

However, when they are dealing with God, these same Christians refuse to invest that much. They still want God to answer their prayers instantly as a click. Some wait for sleep to read the Scriptures, turning the Word of God into a sleeping pill. God cannot accept it. Especially since the devil, *the accuser of the brothers* (**Revelation 12:10**), relies on this disinterest to denounce Christians and attack them.

God is just to all His creatures, even to Satan. The latter asks God for equal measure towards all His creatures, without exception. Satan demands that men be punished in case of wrongdoing like him when he was a shining star, protective cherub in the holy mountain of God. He does not stand a God complacent towards men who mock Him. Indeed, spending hours in front of TV and websites, then devote barely a quarter of an hour to pray and read the Scriptures, attests to an indifference that the devil take advantage of to eagerly accuse Christians.

Remember this answer of Satan to God during Job's hard time:

> *«Satan answered Jehovah and said, skin for skin, yea, **all that a man has he will give for his life**» (**Job 2:4**).*

Satan is aware that a creature of God must invest **all he has for his life**. It is a universal principle which he remembers perfectly, having himself been, for a long time, a brilliant star in the service of God, *cherubim protector and honest* – yes before cutting ties with God, Satan was a worthy servant of God in the heavenly mountain. Christians are not exempt from this principle. The devil knows perfectly well that life is superior to fortune, even if it diverts the attention of its owners elsewhere. Satan exhorts his servants to pay more attention to wealth than life. How many men and women have sacrificed brothers, sisters and parents for money? How many men and women have sold their soul to the devil for better living conditions and glory? Yet Satan, this liar, formally acknowledges before God – whom he cannot deceive – that life has more value than material goods: *all that a man has he will give for his life*.

Christians would do well to remember it. They must show some interest in God's business if they want their prayers to be answered. Today, only a handful of prayers to God are answered because of Christians' disinterest in spirituality. God must be seriously invested.

Christians must be patient. Sometimes it takes a life to confirm the Holy Scriptures. Scripture speaks of Sarah the mother of Isaac, Anne the mother of Samuel, Elizabeth the mother of John the Baptist – these three women were long sterile before giving birth –, Job and many other heroes who went through various misfortunes. In the end, these heroes triumphed despite hardship. Their trials sometimes lasted for years, but in the end, they triumphed.

To achieve triumph, these heroes lived a life of sanctification relentlessly and seriously. They really invested in the Lord. Sara called her husband 'my lord'; Anne came to the temple of God each year and dedicated her firstborn Samuel as offering to the Lord; Elizabeth lived in piety despite her persistent sterility. She ends up giving birth in her old age to the prophet John the Baptist. Job wisely waited for the deliverance of God. All these heroes really took God to heart and triumphed over hardship. Christians must understand that negligence at this level will lead them to a dead end that the devil will take advantage of at their expense.

Many times, I wondered why God hardly answers prayers of nowadays Christian while prayers of Bible heroes were answered quickly. God's reply was that He is waiting for His children to invest in finding solutions before Him. It is then that He will act, and the Christian will glorify Him with the feeling of having really sought the face of God. Because God wants to be part of the life of His children. The latter have the habit of spending hours in TVs and computers. But they want God to respond instantly to their requests, as if connecting to God was as simple as clicking on the Internet. God does not want that. He intends to be invested with the same intensity as when one wants a social promotion or salary increase. It is well known that to achieve these social aims, Christians invest months and years of training. But comes the Scripture and prayer time and they look exhausted. So Satan, the *accuser of the brethren*, rushes to the Lord to block the prayers of the saints because they do not invest enough for their life, the true life, that desired by God. God's wish, which Satan knows well, is *sanctification without which no one will see the Lord*. It is this life of sanctification that opens the windows of heaven. The Christian should be involved in this, remembering this exhortation: **"*Seek first the kingdom of God and His righteousness;* *and all these things*** (wealth and comfort) *shall be added to you"* (**Matthew 6:33**).

Let's end the life of Caviar-Christian and low-cost gospel by investing ourselves deeply in the Lord.

God's tenderness for His children

God reveals Himself deeply to His children

> «*The Spirit searches all things, yea, **the deep things of God***» 1 Corinthians 2:10.

This Scripture quotation indicates the ability of the Spirit to explore the depths of God. It is obvious, we say, because God is also Spirit. But two verses before, an affirmation does intrigue us. The apostle says indeed:

> «*But as it is written, "eye has not seen, nor ear heard," nor has it entered into the heart of man, **"the things which God has prepared FOR those who love Him***»* (1 Corinthians 2:9).

Clearly, when the Spirit explores the depths of God, being God Himself, we must understand that the Spirit does it **FOR** and with *those who love God*. It is truly a walk into the inner apartments of God. It means concretely that God likes to show His inner apartments to those who love Him. Dear reader, should you not be part of those who love God, as God desires you to visit His secret rooms?

What can be found in the inner apartments of God? All. Absolutely everything. Everything related to the creation of God in heaven, on earth, and in waters below the earth. In all its variety therefore. In creating man in His image, God wanted to reveal Himself to this man as He is: God. No less.

What mother would not like to tell everything to her daughter? Which father would not like to reveal everything to his son? It is very important to prepare your offspring for the challenges of life. God does not think less. He wants His children to be well prepared to meet all the challenges of life. He wants His children to know Him. Praying His Father, Jesus said indeed:

> *«And this is life eternal, that **they might know You**, the only true God, and Jesus Christ whom You have sent»* (**John 17:3**).

God will do everything for His children to know Him as long as they are willing and interested. As it comes from God and not man, it is a gift. It is up to man to reach out and avoid missing such an amazing grace.

> To explore the inner apartments of God through the Holy Spirit is to plunge oneself in the inexpressible intentions of God on all matters of life. The more this exercise is carried out, the more the Christian will know God and His will on different matters of life.

Let the Christian, accustomed to this exercise, not be surprised by the instinctive reflexes he will have on realities and facts which surround him. It will happen that, without a rational explanation, the Christian feels internally an opposition to an event, a reality, a behavior, an opinion. It is the result of his many visits into the inner apartments of God. It is after taking into consideration this opposition that God will give him the revelation based on Scripture.

This is why the Christian must never stop sanctifying himself. *Watch and pray!* Says the Lord Jesus Christ. This spiritual watch includes continuous sanctification. By this exercise, the Christian becomes accustomed to the will of God who can first express Himself by instinct before he is given a rational explanation based on Scripture.

The anointing that we have received cannot lie. It is real. It is a very reliable teacher because the Scripture says that we no longer need to be taught because the anointing teaches us everything. It is indeed written:

> *«The anointing which you received from Him abides in you, and* **you do not need anyone to teach you. But as His anointing teaches you concerning all things, and is true and no lie,** *and as He has taught you, abide in Him»* (**1 John 2:27**).

When does God reveal His depths to His children?

This question is both fundamental and simple. Exploring the inner apartments of God has no fixed time. It is a total discretion of the Holy Spirit. The Holy Spirit will seize every opportunity to guide the Christian into the inner apartments of God. The purpose of these visits is to nourish, consolidate the communion, the conscience and the instinct of the Christian.

These visits can be done at any time of the day, during a round trip, during work, in the toilet or in the shower, during walks, during night watches. At all times according to whether the Spirit finds it useful and the Christian available.

The Spirit can focus on a Scripture quotation if He thinks insufficient the Christian's understanding. Since the Spirit explores everything, including the heart of the Christian, He perfectly measures the Christian's understanding of the word of God. The Spirit has received from the Lord the mission to guide the Christian into all truth and to remind him of what Christ has taught:

> *«But the Comforter, the Holy Spirit whom the Father will send in My name, He shall teach you all things and* **bring all things to your remembrance, whatever I have said to you»** **(John 14:26)**.

These moments can multiply to infinity. The Christian will then be able to measure the Lord's love for him through the Holy Spirit. As parents teach their children to provide them with a solid education, a sign of their parental love, so the Spirit wants Christians to know God and the One He sent: Jesus Christ.

The Christian will realize, by himself, how the Spirit is tender, loyal and faithful in love. The touch of the Spirit is as delicious as the oil – ointment –, that is why He is assimilated to the anointing. Those who possess the Spirit of Christ know something about it. God loves His children perfectly.

By fortifying the communion, the conscience and the instinct of the Christian, the latter will know how to recognize the voice of His Master among a thousand. Jesus says indeed:

> *«When the shepherd puts forth his own sheep, he goes before them, and the sheep follow him.*

> *For they know his voice. And they will not follow a stranger, but will flee from him, for they do not know the voice of strangers»* (**John 10:4-5**).

> *«Behold, I stand at the door and knock. If anyone hears My voice and opens the door, I will come in to him and will dine with him and he with Me»* (**Revelation 3:20**).

Dinner is a time souls calmly discuss because after, it's night. So we have time for a talk, the daily constraints being reduced to the bare minimum. In targeting that dinnertime, the Lord indicates how serious He intends to discuss all matters with His children. The Lord treasures these moments because He can then rebuke and encourage for the edification of His Christians to the glory of God the Father.

By visiting the depths of God, we hear the voice of God

Before venturing into the depths of God, I had always been, like many Christians, curious about how God speaks to people. God indeed has many ways to speak to His children. Exploring God's inner apartments is another way of hearing His voice. Whenever you face a situation, the touch of the Spirit, according to your experience of the depths of God, will be the sign that God has spoken to you. The more you practice in exploring the inner apartments of God, the more you will know the will of God on different matters of life. People will be curious to know how God speaks to you: God speaks, that's all.

Should we really ask ourselves how God speaks? God is His own Word that speaks – *In the beginning was the Word, and the Word was with God, **and the Word was God** (**John 1:1**). Is it not the main aim of the Word to emit? The Word voices the will of God as it did in the beginning of all things, before things become reality. It is obvious. God speaks. The Word emits. Just be in the right tune to hear it. We are in the right tune by constantly visiting the depths of God through the Holy Spirit. Amen!

Devote everything to God, including oneself

A revelation of the Holy Spirit on the consecration

I attended Sunday worship, amidst the children of God, when one of the members received from the Spirit a revelation of which here is the content and the translation:

"Suppose a hotelier receives a call from a guest who wants all rooms: I want all rooms, says the guest; I mean A-L-L rooms. What do you mean by ALL rooms? Replies the hotelier: Some rooms are already occupied and I cannot afford to let the occupants out! The customer insists again: I want all rooms. As for the other occupants, if we take just some rooms, we will be a nuisance for them because they do not correspond to us. They will feel completely lost, as in a foreign land, and they will suffer. So I want ALL rooms. Do you have enough money to pay sir? Asks the hotelier again. Yes and I want all rooms."

And the Spirit to reveal the following: *"The customer is Christ; the hotel is the heart of the Christian. Jesus Christ desires all rooms of Christian's heart. He does not want the Christian to devote some rooms to his idols. Jesus Christ wants a whole heart, without exception. Because idols eat away at the ground, weaken the heart that eventually gets away from God."*

This revelation confirms the scriptures where God specifies the following:

> «*You shall love the Lord your God **with all your heart**, and with all your soul, and with all your mind*» (**Matthew 22:37**).

This truth is trumpeted throughout the Scriptures, from the ancient Alliance based on the blood of animals, to the new Alliance in Christ. Consecration consists in submitting everything to God. EVERYTHING: finances, family, health, work, relationships, food, present and future, energy, intelligence, feeling, will, breathing, life and death, even its own precautionary principles.

The idols of the above list are good things because there is nothing wrong with looking after one's finances, family, health, work, relationships, food, present and future. But these things can take God's place in our lives and become idols. The best way to prevent these things from becoming idols is to submit them all to God without regret. God will then break these legitimate ties in the heart of the Christian and take up the entire place.

To submit all these good things to God is to free oneself from their tyranny. That is to say, not to have the same attitude towards them as pagans do. Some concrete examples are necessary to understand what it is about.

If your car breaks down, the natural instinct is to rush to the nearest mechanic. Oh how many women complain that their husbands regard their car as a mistress, as long as they take care of it? The Christian might consider using public transport just to get rid of this idol for a couple of days.

If you are insulted in your workplace, whether the insult comes from the boss or a colleague, the Lord recommends quietness: "*To me is retribution and vengeance*" says the Lord. If the insult is a sneaky insolence coming from the low worker, also rely on the Lord. It is rare that a direct insult comes from a lower worker, but do we ever know?

If your salary does not match the quality of your work, the natural attitude is to ask for a salary increase. If the boss overlooks it, there is no reason to make it an issue, but to put the question to God because, really, the Christian works for God, while his boss is the beneficiary. In due course, the Lord will raise the salary of His child.

If a young sister is treated with indifference by people – or other young women – who look down on her, mocking her appearance, there is no need to rush into a beauty center. The response belongs to the Lord who will make her beautiful and attractive, attractive enough to shut up her opponents.

The essential thing is to build an attitude of effacement and quietness in order to let the Lord act and avenge us. By this attitude, we learn to free ourselves from those idols that eat away at our hearts where God intends to reign unchallenged.

God gave ALL in giving His only begotten Son, so that in return He might get the consecration of ALL our life, as it is written:

> *«Likewise count yourselves also to be truly dead to sin, but **alive to God** through Jesus Christ our Lord»* (**Romans 6:11**).

Consecration consists in giving one's life to God in Christ Jesus. The Christian will be very grateful to Him. In fact, if he wants to recognize it, the man does not know how to manage his own life which more often is out of control. By putting his life in the hands of God, the Christian will discover the mysteries, the heights and depths of the entire creation of God: an exquisite happiness.

Christians can wrongly place a wall between God and their demands

We still remember – for those who read the Scriptures – the visit the angel of the Lord paid to Abraham, to announce him the coming of Isaac from his barren wife Sarah. The patriarch warmly welcomed them.

Here is what the Scriptures relate:

> «*Abraham hastened into the tent to Sarah, and said, make ready quickly three measures of fine meal; knead it, and make cakes. And Abraham ran out to the herd and brought a calf, tender and good. And he gave it to a young man. And he hurried to dress it. And he took butter and milk, and the calf which he had dressed, and set it before them. And he stood by them under the tree, and they ate. And they said to him, where is Sarah your wife? And he said, behold, in the tent. And he said, I will certainly return to you according to the time of life, and lo, Sarah your wife shall have a son. And Sarah heard in the tent door which was behind him*» (**Genesis 18:6-10**).

Imagine that the reception of the patriarch did not match the event. We cannot presume the end result, but no one doubts that the magnitude of the blessings promised would have been considerably reduced.

In the process, these same illustrious visitors went to the nephew of Abraham, Lot, living in Sodom and Gomorrheus. On the other hand, there was a concern about punishments to inflict on Sodom and Gomorrheus. The people of these two cities did nothing to cancel or alleviate the sentence to come. To make it worse, they wanted to outrage the angels of the Lord. This was fatal to them. Not only did they disappear into flames, but Lot lost his wife and the girls he had married to those people. He lost much in the affair because in addition, his two virgin girls had incestuous relations to assure an inheritance to their father: the Moabites and the Ammonites.

Recalling these incidents from history is a warning to Christians to be vigilant not to lose a penny of their blessings.

This chapter was inspired by a mediocre register of the early years of mine in faith. My life did not go the way I wanted. I was far from being a prosperous Christian in all respects while I was overflowing with activities for the Lord. I knew about it and I felt bad. It was then that God sent a prophet to tell me the following: *I (God) know all your prayers, but you have understood nothing.* I received this message as a club blow. Because not only did I know my real discomfort, but also this message confirmed a dream that I had just had. The prophet confirmed the dream as related to the problem. Honestly, I did not understand what the problem was about in details, although the symptoms of spiritual mediocrity were present. The dream simply reflected the image of my opposing all that Christ wanted to do to honor my requests. I prayed, but at the same time, I prevented the Lord from answering my prayers. What a foul I was!

How could I oppose the Lord's action in my favor? I asked myself. I understood the reason of my spiritual life going unsuccessfully. The symptom was there, but I did not understand the root cause. I had to dig deep until a gleam shone in my mind. I simply did not have enough faith in Jesus Christ. More specifically, I did not know what it meant to 'have faith', or rather, I had a very personal translation of that expression. Is not this one the big problems of the Church? Every Christian often has his own translation of the Scriptures. **I asked the Lord for things, but I wanted to solve them for myself instead of letting the Lord act as He pleased**. This is the cause: I was selfish.

Blame it on a life rich in possibilities and means. We ask God for things and, at the same time, we act ourselves hoping that God will support us because of the saying, *"Help yourself and heaven will help you"*. We ask for things and immediately imagine the actions to be taken to make it. We think that it is enough to take action and the Lord will support. I was wrong. If what I ask of God is His will, the action to take and the beginning of the action are incumbent upon Him as much. Yet this is what the Scriptures say:

> *«It is God who **works in you both to will and to do** of His good pleasure»* (**Philippians 2:13**).

It is well said, not only the *willing*, but also the *doing*. Unfortunately, the common practice is that after accepting the Lord's will, we act immediately instead of trusting Him on the right time to start it. My problem was that I used to take action myself and hope for His help to make it a success. In wanting to act myself, I disturbed God's plans. I multiplied personal initiatives and Jesus had only to wait until I collapsed. And when I collapsed, I felt that nothing worked. My spiritual life was mediocre and down.

I had to resign myself to waiting for God's willing and *doing*. Sara had to wait, despite her unfortunate initiatives – such as the coming of God's unwanted son, Ishmael – until the time of God came. Then God allowed a woman of ninety years, with breasts affected by death, to give birth to a son: Isaac, father of Jacob, ancestor of Israel.

By multiplying personal initiatives, after addressing our requests to God, we take the serious risk of frustrating God. By the way, when we multiply the initiatives, what do we do more than pagans? When we finally get a result, pagans can claim it as much and even better. When we multiply prowess, **we do not get the result of our prayers, but the salary of our work**. We can always bless the Lord for that, but we are far from what He wanted. We can even testify that the Lord has answered us, but to be honest, **it is not about grace, but salary**. In Murphy's Law in effect, we show that the more we try things, the more chances we have to succeed. Christians must not take this for the answer, but as the result of a series of attempts, one of which proved to be successful. Pagans do the same but do not praise God.

We must wait wisely for God's action in response to our prayers. There is no prayer to be done when one has the means to perform an action. If we pray, then wait patiently for God's answer. Let's wait for the grace of God. Grace means there is no work to rely on, otherwise it is not a grace that we get, but the salary of our efforts.

It took me years of research to understand, finally, the attitude that God expects from the repentant sinner.

- **Firstly**, we must understand and admit that Adam's sin totally disqualified his descendants from any possibility of pleasing God in their bodies, a body cursed for being sentenced to return to the dust. From the immortal he was originally, the man was sentenced to death in the Garden of Eden: *"... until you return to the dust from which you were created ..."*. All that man can obtain from this body of death, now, is nothing but defilement. By eating from the tree of knowledge of good and evil, in rebellion, man has become capable of good and evil. God rejects both because good and evil come from the same root. Unfortunately in his thought, man feels that he pleases God when he does well, and that he displeases God when he does bad. This is partly true. Partly only. Indeed, by saying, *"Let the dead bury their dead,"* Jesus declared dead and useless all that emanates from the natural man, for God is holy and rejects what has failed. This is why, in the Scriptures, God always rejects what has failed. And when He maintains the ultimate goal despite the failure, He makes sure that the new process is immaculate, flawless. That is, He replaces the process that had failed by a new process, while those whom He maintains in the transition pass through purification. This is why the Israelites were to purify themselves with the blood of animals after sinning, while the clay vessels on which the unclean persons sat were broken. Such is the holiness of God and what it requires to be holy. The man having failed, he was rejected; and all that emanates from him is defiled. That is why Jesus came to endorse this condemnation by becoming the last Adam (**1 Corinthians 15:45**) who dies on the cross, sinking all the Adamic offspring with Him, before resurrecting as a life-giving Being. By Jesus' death on the cross, all the Adamic offspring was judged including the last person to be born at the end of time.

- **Secondly**, it is because the Christian has been purified and possesses the Holy Spirit that he can address his prayers to God. However, the processes used by man in the fulfillment of God's will must be holy. But man wrongly believes that all good is approved of God. Scripture declares that even our most righteous deeds are defilement before God (**Isaiah 64:6 or 64:5**).

Here is the crucial point of what we say: when the Christian receives an order from God, or when God reveals His will, Christian must always declare himself irrelevant because he lives in a body of sin, sentenced to return to dust. **He must confess to God his inability to honor God's will by personal efforts**. That's not all. Following this acceptation of incompetence, he must thank the Lord for having chosen him to achieve His goal. Then he must finally ask God to act as He alone knows how to make it successfully. If the man skips these precautions, to act without consideration, he will face serious disappointments. On the other hand, by declaring himself irrelevant, God will take note of his submission and operate in him *the doing* according to His benevolent purpose. The drama of many believers is to impute to their talents the reason why God solicited them. God will never trust our natural capacities and talents. No prophet of the old covenant was able to say why God chose him. Talent can be used if God wishes, but is not required. The angels who are at His service are well equipped to do His will. Joseph did not need natural talents to reveal to the Egyptian Pharaoh the famine that was going to strike his kingdom for many years. David did not need talents to strike the giant Goliath. Daniel did not need talents to reveal to the king of Babylon his scary dream. All trusted God alone and not their natural talents which, let us say, did not stand compare to their opponents. David, for example, was far from having the warrior skills, as a teenager he was, in front of General Goliath who had learned the best fighting techniques

> since childhood. In the same way, Joseph was nothing compared to the Egyptian priests and alchemists whose techniques of mummification have been conserving human bodies for several millennia.

The Christian must therefore learn to humble himself before God, in all things, to see the plan of God fulfilled by him. If he relies on his own intelligence and strength – talents – God will resist him because this Christian will certainly congratulate himself for the success. God does not wish it because *He will not give His glory to anyone.*

All things have become new to him who believes

> «*If anyone is in Christ, that one is a new creature; old things have passed away; behold, **all things have become new**»* (**2 Corinthians 5:17**).

For His newly created Christians, God has provided for the renewal of all things. Christians must expect everything to change in their life and surrounding. What is the magnitude of the change? There is no formal answer to this question. Let us not forget that here it is the Spirit of God who expresses Himself through Apostle Paul. God did not specify the scope and depth of the change concerning *'all things'*. From there, it would be inappropriate to gamble. It is advisable to take it literally. As *'all things have become new'*, let us take the Lord God literally. All means ALL without exception.

Everything can change for the one who has believed: surrounding, job, talents, passions, physical appearance (size, skin and look), future, parents – yes, a Christian can have new parents for life. To a question about His biological parents, Jesus answered:

> *«For whoever shall do the will of My Father in heaven, the same is My brother and sister and mother»* (**Matthew 12:50**).

Unfortunately, even after believing, many Christians keep maintaining pre-conversion thoughts and prejudices. This is a serious mistake. Everything can change in the life of the new convert. He should stick to this position of faith without doubting. It is then that he will see the glory of God. Surprise is now part of the life of God's children. As much as the twelve disciples went from surprise to another while accompanying Jesus on the earth, Christians will be greatly surprised in their new lives.

The Christian should therefore prepare for many changes in his life. There is no way out. There can't be. If he resists, he will be like the one Jesus refers to in the following words: *He who will preserve his life will lose it* (**Matthew 10:39**). The Christian must follow Jesus wherever He goes. He is now a temporary immigrant in this world, as King David himself said in his days.

These changes can be painful. It does not matter; the Christian must persevere in obedience. The beginnings are always difficult; after, things go easier because the Christian is already vaccinated against hardship. It is God who breaks the bridges with the surrounding world in order to prepare for the future rapture of the Christian. Let us remember Lot's wife, who had so much trouble turning the page of her past that she was turned into a statue of salt. In wanting to preserve her life – in the world – she lost it.

Concretely, when the Christian finds that the Lord is leading him with horse reins, he must not resist. In His grace and mercy, the Lord has often arranged to get all doors closed but one for the Christian. It's up to him to seize that one. Often, when there are many choices, we are embarrassed and at the end we wonder if we have made the right decision. By closing all doors but one, the Lord is helping His Christians walk to victory. Glory to God!

Christian who is reluctant to change is like wine that has never been decanted during its making. Such wine keeps its lees, which greatly reduces its quality. Experts will take note and downgrade it. When the Christian resists change, his perfume does not change before the Almighty who will show His disappointment before Christ. Not a good thing for this Christian.

The inheritance of the Christian: The windows of Heaven

Christians must look up to heaven and not turn down that great asset at their disposal: the windows of heaven. It is hopeless and narrow-minded to believe that the windows of heaven will only be available after the rapture, or at the end of time. It is not fair to think that way because God has already given us a glimpse of these windows during Jesus' earthly journey, and even before this journey, during prophets' time.

Let us understand well what the *windows of heaven* mean here. Basically, it is the resources of heaven, not present on the earth. They are inaccessible to men, even equipped with modern extraction tools. No map can locate them because they are simply not locatable on the earth. But they are present in heaven. It was these resources that poured out on the Israelites like the manna from heaven. The Lord did not gather all the bakers on the earth to feed the Israelites in the desert. These are the windows of heaven that poured manna into the desert. It was a historic and extraordinary event because of the forty years pilgrimage of the Israelite people in the desert.

But let us remember that the Israelite people, after having settled on the promised land, had continued to benefit from windows of heaven in other forms. This is the case of the angels slaying the soldiers of a powerful enemy army in front of a diminished Israelite army (**2 Kings 19:35**). This is the case of the Lord returning enemy soldiers against each other until they are totally destroyed (**Judges 7:22**).

Furthermore, let us remember Jesus Christ stopping the storm, multiplying bread, raising the dead, walking on water and performing various miracles. These are operations involving the heavens, without any recourse to the resources of the earth. But Jesus promised that *His disciples would also perform the miracles He had performed; even more,* given the limited time of His earthly pilgrimage – three years. What can we conclude of all this? The only possible inference is that Christians must also rely on the windows of heaven to achieve their goals.

Honestly, the resources of the earth are not enough for the happiness of Christians. The latter must open their intelligence and reach out to an available inheritance: the windows of heaven. Jesus resorted to it. They too must resort to it. Oh may the Lord helps them and open their mind to seize these opportunities.

It is unfortunate that the intelligence of Christians is heavily science-based in assessing resources on the earth. Christians have become used to it, like the world, to foresee the future. Humans are not wrong in estimating Earth's potential and designing the programs of the future. They cannot go beyond that. But Christians have the windows of heaven at their disposal. They can rely on it when needed. Let them pray God in the name of Jesus and they will see the glory of God.

In this regard, the attitude of Christians when facing diseases is close to pagan mentality. They act exactly like unbelievers.

We must admit that the resources of this world are not enough for the happiness of Christians to whom God has promised nations and a scepter of iron to rule them. Like Jesus stopping the storm, multiplying bread, raising the dead and healing various diseases, the Christian really needs the windows of heaven to pour over the earth. It should not be surprising that the windows of heaven are opened to Christians. Did God not declare that *the earth was cursed for the sake of man? That it shall also bring forth thorns and thistles to him?* (**Genesis 3:17-19**). How can one imagine that God can rely on such a confused and unstable resource to feed His children? Absurd.

We insist again that the magnitude of blessings of the Christian far exceeds all earth resources. If the Christian relies on the resources of this world, he will face rivalry from men and women who will give him a huge fight, even if this Christian would prevail at the end. The Christian needs the windows of heaven to open to him. Jesus resorted to it during His earthly journey, declaring that after His departure, His disciples would also perform the miracles He had performed, even more because His mission lasted only three years, whereas the Christians have their whole life to go. So let's not spit on such an asset based on clear promises.

God has promised the windows of heaven. Let us grab it without waiting for after-death-life. Here we go, amen!

The greatest inheritance: The throne of God

> «*To him that is victorious, to him **will I give to sit with Me on My Throne**, even as I was victorious, and sat down with My Father on His Throne*» **Revelation 3:21 (Bible Murdoch)**.

The Throne of God is by far the highest inheritance that God can promise to obedient Christians. The Lord has promised many things to Christians. For example the payback, up to a hundredfold, of all the investments made in His name, now in this time, and eternal life in the world to come (**Mark 10:30**).

However the message of **Revelation 3:21** above is unequivocal. The Lord promises the victors nothing less than His Throne. Why would the Christian target less? If you win the lottery, will you take only a part of it because the whole fortune seems too big to handle? Let us remember Jesus recovering twelve baskets of breads out of the miraculous multiplication of five loaves and two fishes that fed thousands of people. Everyone being satiated, did Jesus think that it was no longer useful to worry about leftover bread? No, He collected it. Therefore we must not diminish the promise of the

Lord in connection with His throne. He promises it to the victors. Then only one choice must be on target to Christians: the throne. Do not spit in the soup (throne) of the Lord. May Christians rejoice that Jesus Christ offers them as much as His heavenly throne in His grace.

Let's be realistic and wise. The inheritance of God is plural and includes many goods available to His heirs. There is one that is special, the most cherished of all. This is, no doubt, His Throne. This Throne is the most coveted of all times by the devil, aka the shining star, aka Satan, aka the ancient serpent, aka the blood red dragon, aka Beelzebub. Created a shining star, protective cherub, with the most beautiful appearance ever given to a creature, Satan wanted to rise above the stars of God to invest the Throne of the Almighty. He was rebuke by God: "***Yet you are a man and not God**, though you set your heart as the heart of God*" (**Ezekiel 28: 2**).

Christians must understand the reason for the devil's continued harassment against them. The devil has read **Revelation 3:21** and is furious with Christians who have been promised what he covets most. 'Why men (created inferior to angels) but him?' is his main concern. His goal is to keep as many men as possible away from the trophy he had so coveted that he was sentenced to hell for eternity, he and his fallen angels.

Christians should not spit in this soup marked with the seal of God: His Throne. The devil is very serious and still cherishes the hope that a clumsiness of man – like that of Adam and Eve – will give him a pole to this throne. If he succeeded in fooling the man – who was created king at the beginning, but the devil supplanted him and became the *prince of this world* – he hopes for another opportunity to rob man of the right to sit on the throne of God. At least he hopes to become prince of the eternal kingdom of God and escape the hell that is reserved for him.

Christians must block the way. The error of Adam and Eve must not happen again. Christians then understand the categorical refusal of God to any relationship with the enemy and his spells: sorcery, white or black magic, horoscope, divination practices, conjuring, vampirism, worship and consultation of the dead, etc.

God indeed says to the Israelite people:

> *«When you come to the land which Jehovah your God gives you, you shall not learn to do according to the abominations of those nations.* **There shall not be found among you anyone who makes his son or his daughter to pass through the fire, or that uses divination, an observer of clouds, or a fortune-teller, or a witch, or a charmer, or a consulter with familiar spirits, or a wizard, or one who calls to the dead. For all that do these things are an abomination to Jehovah.** *And because of these abominations Jehovah your God drives them out from before you»* (**Deuteronomy 18:9-12**).

Access the invisible riches that only God sees

No need to recall that the disciples of Jesus Christ were regularly surprised by His miracles. One of the reasons for all this is that they did not imagine a man could do the miracles that Jesus did.

Remember that Jesus turned water into wine. He broke the storm, multiplied bread for the multitude who followed him, raised Lazarus, and so on. In other words, the disciples of Jesus could not see what He, the Lord, saw. They were surprised. If Jesus multiplied bread, it was because He saw this bread, not the disciples. If Jesus turned water into wine, it was because He saw this wine, not the disciples.

Honestly, these types of miracles were the rule, not the exception during Christ's journey on the earth. He says indeed:

> «*He who believes on Me, **the works that I do he shall do also**, and greater works than these he shall do, because I go to My Father*» (**John 14:12**).

How sad to discover that many end-time Christians have little interest in this truth of the Scriptures! Astonishing. It is well written though, without a shadow of a doubt. The reality is far from the promise of the Lord. Oh Lord! Help this sinful and careless generation. Miracles have become the exception among Christians. In fact, the few testimonies heard here and there are flies compared to the miracles of Jesus of Nazareth and during apostle time. Christians are therefore far from the truth according to the gospel of Christ.

We reiterate that doing the works that Jesus did, or even greater ones, means that the Christian must rely on the windows of heaven that only God sees, not the Christian. Not seeing these windows with eyes does not mean that they are non-existent. The Christian is invited to bring them down for the glory of God. He must insist and recall the promise of God, rather than resign himself to the current status quo so distressing.

The Scriptures recount a scene where the prophet Elisha, man of God, showed his assistant the chariots of fire of God around. The servant trembled at the sight of the enemy chariots encamped around Israel, but Elisha saw the chariots of fire of God ready to overthrow the enemy:

> «*The servant of the man of God (Elisha) arose early and went out. And, behold, an army surrounded the city, and horses and chariots. And his servant said to him, Alas, my master! What shall we do? And he answered, do not fear, **for those with us are more than those***

> *with them. And Elisha prayed and said, I pray You, Jehovah, open his eyes so that he may see. And Jehovah opened the eyes of the young man, and he saw. And behold, **the mountain was full of horses and chariots of fire round about Elisha**» (**2 Kings 6:15-17**).*

He who is in you (Christians) *is greater than he who is in the world*, says Apostle John (**1 John 4:4**). May Christians fill themselves with courage to claim the windows of heaven that are within reach. It will be only one more thing in their life of piety and sanctification. Christians really need it in the furnace and embers that rage around.

The status of the Christian: a heavenly crown prince

Scripture strongly supports that Christians are princes of God. How can they be heirs of God and joint-heirs with Christ without being princes? To inherit a king, one must be his crown prince.

God, the King of kings, cannot therefore promise Christians His inheritance if they are not His crown princes. Christians are therefore the crown princes of God. In all honesty, the heir of the King of kings can only be prince of princes, not less. It is not superfluous for a Christian to take himself for the prince of princes. When the princes of this world are *terrestrial crown princes*, he, the Christian, is *celestial crown prince* because his Father the King of kings sits in heavenly places.

How sad it is to see Christians living as losers in the world, looking like they had gone missing or regretted having chosen the opprobrium of Christ?

Several scenes of life make it possible to affirm that Christians dishonor the Lord by their complex of inferiority towards the great ones of this world, whereas they are actually above the crown princes of the earth. They are especially above the crown princes of England, Spain, Sweden, Saudi Arabia and Japan, to name only the most famous of today. Jesus was so scary that Herod wanted to see Him. Really Jesus was greater than all the crown princes of the earth. He was the King of Jews, not less. Apostle John did so many miracles that the Roman emperor exiled him on Patmos island, fearing for his throne. There Jesus paid John a visit that fueled the book of Revelation (**Revelation 1:9**). The emperor therefore found Apostle John superior to all the crown princes of Roman Empire. Should you not, Christians, regard you as the heavenly crown princes? It is far from being exaggerated. Apostle John was to the point of shaking an ancient empire as powerful as the United States today. You are no way less than him, are you?

Let us remember the Jew Mordecai facing Amalekite Haman from the Book of Esther. In short, we are in the midst of deported peoples in a kingdom of one hundred and twenty-seven provinces. It is certainly the greatest kingdom on the earth at that time. The Jews are also there as deportees. Haman is the prime minister from the deportation, while Mordecai is a deported Jew working at the Royal Conciergerie. Scripture relates that the Jew Mordecai never pledged allegiance to Amalekite Haman, the prime minister of King Ahasuerus. This irreverent attitude annoyed the prime minister, who decided to put an end to the insolent. History will remember that Haman, rather than punishing Mordecai alone, decided to decimate the entire Jewish race. God acted in favor of Mordecai, and Haman was hanged on the gallows he had prepared for Mordecai. This event is celebrated worldwide every year by Jews people as Purim celebration.

Why did Mordecai refuse to bow to Haman, whereas Scripture recommends to submit to the authorities established by God (**Romans 13:1**)? The answer certainly lies in the fact that Haman was Amalekite, of that race that God had decided to exterminate for opposing the exit of Israel from Egypt (**Exodus 17:8, 1 Samuel 15:2**). Thus Mordecai, aware of his status, could submit to all the royal authorities except Haman. God gave him right, because Haman was finally executed and Mordecai promoted Prime Minister.

There are many cases in life where Christians should not let themselves down because of their status as crown princes of God, the King of Kings. The way may differ from one another because, in the above narration, Mordecai's resistance was sly for fear of offending the royal edict in Haman's favor. Haman suffered in secret and understood what was going on. He says indeed: *"Yet all this (wealth and glory) avails me nothing as long as I see Mordecai the Jew sitting at the king's gate"* (**Esther 5:13**).

Some cases will help us understand what a crown crince of God really is.

The Christian must be inspired by the crown princes of the earth

Have you often observed the behavior of the crown princes of the earth? They are very confident about their future because their father – or mother – sits on the throne. In fact, which sovereign did never care about his succession in quantity and quality? It is obvious that every sovereign has always had in mind that his heirs meet the requirements of a reign as prestigious as his or even more.

What training will a crown prince not undertake to ascend the throne? Answer: the best of the kingdom no matter the topic.

God does not act differently toward His heirs, the Christians, joint-heirs with Christ. God ensures that Christians receive a quality training that allows them to sit firmly on the heavenly throne.

Are Christians aware of it? The whole question lies there. The Christian must therefore become aware of his true status as Crown Prince of the Celestial Throne. Targeting lower means, for a prince, to live like a commoner. It is selfishness and lese-majesty against the Almighty God.

Jesus did not honor king Herod's invitation

It is well known, and Scripture confirms it, that Herod wanted to meet Jesus during His earthly journey. The answer of Jesus was radical:

> *«You go and tell that fox (Herod), behold, today and tomorrow, I cast out demons and I complete cures, and the third day I will be finished»* (**Luke 13:32**).

Are Christians aware that they must reproduce the life of Jesus Christ? The Scripture says:

> *«He who says he abides in Christ ought himself also to walk **even as He walked**»* (**1 John 2:6**).

How many Christians today rush to the slightest desire of the princes of the city? Christians do not realize how much they publicly humiliate the Lord of glory by running after the princes of the city. As if being in the service of the Lord Jesus Christ is an ungrateful job. Are there not many pastors who hope for a prince visiting their church? Are there not many of them to reserve the highest seat of the church to these distinguished guests? What a shame! The Lord Jesus is thus reduced to the lower rank, since His servants run after the crumbs that fall under the table of the princes of this world. Satan is thankful to them.

How will the world not think that Christians are of lower social rank, always looking for tax and customs exemptions. Is Jesus running out of money so that His servant may not pay local taxes? Unless rendering services of public utility, such as teaching and medical care, there is no reason for the servants of God, in their job, to avoid all sort of taxes. Even the place of worship should not be haggled with the authorities. If Christians believe that they must meet at a given place, according to a certain comfort, that they ask the Lord to do so, and the Lord will grant them, without the local authority taking advantage of it. The windows of heaven will show as in the days of Jesus Christ, to the glory of God the Father.

Jesus did not pray anyone to believe Him as the Son of God

Jesus did ask but did not pray anyone to believe Him as the Son of God. Christians must question their attitude in the world regarding the glory of God. When Jesus taught *to eat His flesh and drink His blood,* Scripture says that many of His followers left angry. Such public disavowal could have caused the Lord to cool down and compromise. But what did the Lord do? He openly challenged those who remained in these terms:

> *«Do you (the twelve apostles) also wish to go away?»* (**John 6:67**).

In other words, Jesus made them understand that they were free to follow those who left. Such an attitude can be viewed as arrogant. No, Jesus knew that He was the only begotten Son of God – before the resurrection. He was therefore the Unique Crown Prince of the Heavenly Kingdom. He could simply not lower Himself to pray his listeners to follow Him.

Christians must therefore review their attitude. They do not have to pray people to believe that Jesus Christ is the Son of God. If anyone refuses to believe, the Christian moves on and remains in prayer. But supplication is totally forbidden, for example crying to obtain the yes of the evangelized. Jesus simply does not agree with this method. It is to make the young convert believe that Jesus needs crowds to be a true Lord. Unfortunately, the reckless attitude of many Christians let the world think that Jesus Christ is a little Lord who needs people around Him. Let's not be surprised by the poor quality of many conversions. People have simply received a cheap gospel, unworthy of the Lord of glory.

Can today's pastor openly condemn sin and ask sinners to put money in the wallet of the church? It is disrespectful to these listeners isn't? Alas, to prevent churches from emptying and church's coffers from diminishing, many pastors have lowered their preaching against sin. Sin can then spread into hypocrisy in the church: adultery, fornication, gossip, theft, lies, etc.

It is better to have a church with few members, and true Christians, than a church full of Sunday Christians, including ferocious beasts, traitors, and ravening wolves. *"Better is a little with the fear of Jehovah than great treasure and tumult with it"* (**Proverbs 15:16**).

Jesus did not yield to His biological parents to the detriment of the Heavenly Father

We cannot ignore the importance of family relationships in one individual's life. Christians are no exception. They are affected by family relationships: father, mother, brother, sister, cousin, nephew, etc. Many Christians have thus abandoned the Lord out of love for their biological parents.

But Jesus did not give in to His biological parents. Several scenes of Scripture attest to this.

Jesus refused to honor His mother and brothers when preaching. Scripture relates the following:

> *«Then His brothers and His mother came. And standing outside, they sent to Him, calling Him. And the crowd sat about Him, and they said to Him, behold, Your mother and Your brothers are outside seeking for You. And He answered them, saying, who is My mother, or My brothers? And He looked around on those*

> *who sat about Him, and said, behold My mother and My brothers! For whoever does the will of God, the same is My brother and My sister and My mother»* (**Mark 3:31-35**).

To better grasp the context of the event, it must be remembered that the biological family of Jesus Christ lived in Nazareth, Galilee, tens of kilometers from Jerusalem. To come from so far could only be done in delegation. The reason was surely to reprimand and bring back this rebellious Son whom the Jews threatened to kill. What could be more natural for a family to worry about the fate of one of them, because of noises of arrests that were circulating against him (**Mark 3:21**).

Jesus also knew that His biological family had certainly traveled tens of kilometers to Jerusalem in His footsteps. He did not find it enough to derogate from the mission His Father had entrusted to him. And as it was the case, on many occasions when Jesus reminded Joseph and Mary – His earthly parents – that He had to obey His Heavenly Father, Jesus took no notice of the family's request. Jesus did not worry about what will be said. It was His right to do the will of His Father in heaven, regardless of the opinion of men and women, even of His earthly parents.

Jesus denied His mum Mary to be glorified by the world. The Scripture says:

> *«And it happened as He spoke these things, a certain woman of the company lifted up her*

*voice and said to Him, blessed is the womb that bore You, and the breasts which You have sucked. But He said, no; rather, **blessed are they who hear the word of God and keep it**»* (**Luke 11:27-28**).

In the world, there is nothing wrong with the mother of a high personality being honored. It's very common. But Jesus, in the above narration, does not agree with it regarding His biological mother. He rebuked the admirer (a woman) by making her understand that only those who listened and obeyed the word of God deserved such honor. We can also see that it was an admirer woman desiring to remind the crowd the saying that *behind a great man, there is a great mother*. This look is not without calculation. However, for Jesus, it was out of question that His mission be affected by precepts of laudable appearance without any real use in sanctification.

These two examples provide us with a guideline on the attitude that Christians should have toward their biological parents. But our experience proves that we are far from the divine standard. Many Christians still cannot balance things between the will of the flesh and the will of God. Jesus says yet:

*«If anyone comes to Me and **does not hate his father and mother and wife and children and brothers and sisters, yes, and his own life also**, he cannot be My disciple»* (**Luke 14:26**).

It is unfortunate that this warning does not echo among Christians. It is surprising and a pity that Christian leaders' obsession with filling the churches, to look good, is at the expense of God's commandments, as if the main purpose were to make everyone happy. The strategy of accustoming Christians to church attendance, and then revealing uncomfortable truths to them, does not come from God, because they are faced with a fait accompli. It's cunning, and the Lord hates to bring people into His fold by cunning. They will immediately left after the truth is revealed, feeling that they have been trapped. They could then curse the Lord instead of praising Him. The message of salvation must be preached without complacency, even if the listener is shocked. The gospel of Jesus Christ is not a flattery, it is a matter of life and death. We do not have to flatter the world. Jesus did not flatter anyone. Christians should follow His example.

Jesus says Himself:

> *«For which of you, intending to build a tower, does not sit down first and count the cost, whether he may have enough to finish it; lest perhaps, after he has laid the foundation and is not able to finish, all those seeing begin to mock him, saying, this man began to build and was not able to finish. Or what king, going to make war against another king, does not first sit down and consult whether he is able with ten thousand to meet him who comes against him with twenty thousand? Or else, while the other is still a great way off, he sends a delegation and asks conditions of peace.* **So**

then, everyone of you who does not forsake all his possessions, he cannot be My disciple» (**Luke 14:28-33**).

The conclusion of this saying of Christ demonstrates the seriousness of repentance. The two examples mentioned in this saying refer to the need for thoughtful preparation before any initiative. Clearly, the disciple must really know what he is doing before taking the decisive step towards the Lord. One does not make disciples of Christ by resorting to trickery. It is necessary to reveal as much as possible, to the future convert, that faith is a very serious affair. It's a new real life that will begin.

The earthly Church is the body of a heavenly Being seated at the right of the Father: Jesus Christ

This truth is highlighted by the Scriptures. The Church is the body of Christ who sat at the right of the Heavenly Father, where He waits for His enemies to become His footstool (**Mark 12:36**).

At the end of His earthly journey, Jesus asked the Father to sanctify His disciples who, being no longer of this world, had to live in the midst of the world. Jesus says indeed:

> «*I have given them (disciples) Your word, and the world has hated them because **they are not of the world, even as I am not of the world. I do not pray for You to take them out of the world, but for You to keep them from the evil. They are not of the world, even as I am not of the world.** Sanctify them through Your truth. Your word is truth. As You have sent Me into the world, even so I have sent them into the world. And I sanctify Myself for their sakes, so that they also might be sanctified in truth*» (**John 17:14-19**).

It is therefore undeniable that the body of Christians, the Church, is the body of a Being who now lives in heaven, at the right of the Father. Jesus Christ is thus today a Celestial Being whose Body – Church – dwells on the earth. As Jesus Christ is the Head of this Body, we say, to be honest, that the Church is a body whose Head lives in heaven. As the head and body of a being are united and share the same (divine) nature, **the Church is a heavenly body living on the earth**.

Hence the essential and obvious question: How will the Church, that heavenly (divine nature) body, live on the earth?

How will the Church, this heavenly body, live on the earth?

Christians are called to realize that they are a heavenly body living on the earth. As such, they must act accordingly by following the heavenly laws. This statement may give rise to reasonable concerns. But deep down, Scripture says that salvation *by grace through faith* does not depend on Christians, but is a gift from God (**Ephesians 2:8**). This means that Christians do not have to gamble on the fate awaiting them in the sheepfold of Christ. The sheepfold of Christ, the Church, belongs to Christ who disposes of it as He pleases. If Christ had made sure that the Church is a heavenly body living on the earth, we must accept that the Church is governed by the laws of heaven. It's up to Christ to handle this business, not the Christians. Jesus has never said, nor Scriptures, that Christians will not have issue. To be honest, worries and anxieties of all kinds are part of the Christian's burden. But the solution belongs to Christ who promised never to abandon His Christians to themselves. Christians must therefore remain calm despite worries.

Why not rejoice, on the other hand, that the Church of Christ be governed by the laws on celestial bodies? Christians should rejoice because it would mean that laws and armies of heaven are at their disposal. Christians should not hesitate to appeal to heaven's laws as necessary. That is why Jesus could interrupt the storm, raise the dead, open the eyes of the blind, multiply bread, walk on water, etc. Jesus therefore regularly appealed to the forces and laws on celestial bodies. We have summarized them above using the term *'Windows of heaven'*.

James had understood this well by saying this:

> *«Every good gift and every perfect gift **is from above** and comes down from the Father of lights, with Whom is no variableness nor shadow of turning»* (**James 1:17**).

> *«But if you have bitter jealousy and strife in your hearts, do not glory and lie against the truth. **This is not the wisdom coming down from above, but is earthly, sensual, devilish.** For where envying and strife are, there is confusion and every foul deed. **But the wisdom that is from above is first truly pure, then***

peaceable, gentle, easy to be entreated, full of mercy and good fruits, without partiality and without hypocrisy» (**James 3:14-17**).

By these words, James invites Christians to set the course for heavenly gifts (**James 1:17**) and wisdom from above (**James 3:17**). The world shares scientific discoveries through primary, secondary, higher and vocational education. It is obvious that Christians, receiving these teachings, are accustomed to address issues through terrestrial solutions. But the Lord of glory invites them to rely on the laws of heaven. It is the Lord who affirms it. It is up to Christians to reach out instead of doubting it.

Christians are therefore invited to seek the windows of heaven to live in this world. This is what Jesus specifies by punctuating many of His messages by "*so that the world may see your good works and glorify your Father who is in heaven*". How will the world glorify the heavenly Father if Christians perform acts like everybody? God wants Christians to bring in the heavenly laws and the windows of heaven on the earth. Thus the world, stupefied, can only bow before God the Father. Amen!

It does not matter what the world will think. Jesus performed his miracles in the amazement of the disciples and pagans. This stupefaction did not dissuade Him from continuing His mission. Jesus said that His disciples would do the miracles that He had done, even greater ones because His mission on the earth was to end early. Christians are therefore invited not to be intimidated by astonishment and what will be said about it. They must honor the word of the Lord. The Christian must dare because the Lord invites him to do so. It is Jesus Christ who has the right to deal with the consequences of the actions that He calls Christians to perform. Do not let Him down.

As part of a Celestial Being, the Church (body) of Christ is immaculate

Having demonstrated that the Church is the body of a Celestial Being – that means that the Church is truly a celestial body – yet residing on the earth, we must insist and say that according to the Scriptures, the Church is immaculate, without sin, stainless. Its members do not sin. The apostle John says it bluntly (**1 John 3:9**). Otherwise Jesus Christ, the Head of this body, would be a sinner. But Jesus Christ is immaculate. He doesn't sin and never did He sin. He is not a sinner because no one can sin and stand at the right of the heavenly Father.

The members of the Church must therefore practice sanctification relentlessly. All its members must be baptized with water. It is sad to meet non-baptized members in churches, some going as far as leading spiritual activities. It's certainly the fault of careless leaders who let things get that far. Shame on them.

The Church does not belong to the leaders or pastors. These are called by the true Head, Jesus Christ, to perform specific tasks. They must conform the Church to the standards of Christ. Every member of the Church must be led into a serious process of conformity with the standard of Christ. Every Christian must be baptized with water and receive the gift of the Holy Spirit. This is the standard. It does not matter if the process takes long, it should not be interrupted as long as there are non-compliant members. It is important to point this out because the Church of Jesus Christ is immaculate even as His Head, the Lord, is immaculate and holy. Jesus said, *Go and make disciples, baptize them.* The Church and its leaders should not fail nor compromise.

Leaders should tremble at the idea of leading a church that does not conform to Christ's standard, if at least they fear Him. They must really get down to the task of ensuring a normal church. Otherwise, we will have sick churches with all kinds of disabilities. The members of the church will lose the real landmarks. The windows of heaven could see their taps greatly reduced, which would not be to the advantage of Christians. And the world will not glorify our heavenly Father. Oh Lord Help us!

Access to the windows of heaven

God has always made His children understand that He not only holds the key to the windows of heaven, but He also puts these windows at their disposal.

Let us remember Moses moving towards the Red Sea with the Israelite people recently freed from Egyptian bondage. The Pharaoh took the pretext that the Israelite people had lost their way to launch the army to bring them back. But God separated the Red Sea in two, and Israel was able to cross on foot, while the Pharaoh's army suffered a monumental defeat. Never in the past had such an event happened on the earth. God had just sent His angels to crush the Pharaoh's army.

It was the same when Joshua, successor of Moses, wanted to cross the Jordan river with the people. God divided the river in two and Israel was able to cross.

As recalled in this book, Jesus did miracles based on the windows of heaven, promising that His disciples would do the same and even more.

A Christian life outside the windows of heaven does not impress the world

> «*Let your light so shine before men **that they may see your good works and glorify your Father who is in heaven***». **Matthew 5:16**.

It is a claim of Jesus, recalled several times during His earthly journey: Christians must impress the world with their works so that the world may glorify the heavenly Father.

But how to impress the world if Christians do everything like the world? The use of the windows of heaven is therefore unavoidable. And it is the will of God that Christians resort to it, not only exceptionally, but on a regular basis.

As such, Christians must dare and not shut themselves within the boundaries of said 'academically correct' that the world has set as standard. No act of Jesus was academically correct. We do not raise the dead already buried as was the case of Lazarus. One could still raise a man who has just been declared dead. Men can then blame his death for a probable medical error. But to raise a man buried four days ago, in the process of decomposition, is really extraordinary.

Christians must dare in their prayers and ask for miracles. It is sad that many churches send their patients to the hospital, without having exhausted the ways of the Lord. They claim to pray for the doctor to treat the patient. But if the prayers of the saints have not saved the sick, how will medicine save him? Is not this hypocrisy? Far from us any intention to discredit hospitals. They are very useful. But as much as the apostle Paul complained that Corinthian Christians submitted their differences to the righteousness of men, even though they possessed the Spirit of God in them, as much it may be distressing to see churches channeling their sick to hospitals, while they hold the healing power promised by the Lord of glory. Shame on us!

Do not misunderstand the Scriptures. Many preachings invite Christians to sobriety. This sobriety is a spiritual lifestyle. We must submit to each other because each Christian has received a different gift. We must also avoid overeating. Eating three portions a day rather than one can expose to certain physical diseases – overweight – and psychic – gluttony. But the opening of the windows of heaven does not call into question these precautions on sobriety. We mean here that limiting our hope on human capacities is not faith. The Lord invites us to open the windows of heaven, so please do not let down that possibility:

> «*Test Me now with this, says Jehovah of hosts,* ***to see if I will not open the windows of heaven for you,*** *and pour out a blessing for you,* ***until there is not enough room***» (**Malachi 3:10**).

Increasing access to the windows of heaven

Even if the Lord asks to be petitioned on any favorable occasion or not, Christians must be careful not to grieve the Holy Spirit who resides in them. Christians must live in the piety and sanctification that pleases the Lord.

Addressing requests to God, while living in sin, is like an employee who expects a salary increase while ruining the assets of his company. Will he be honored by his boss? No, he will be severely punished and sacked.

Piety is a must if you want to open the windows of heaven on the earth. Christians must become familiar with the blood of Christ as the best detergent for purifying their sins. Then they must stop the carnal tendencies that irritate the Lord. The carnal tendencies concern the dead works or any act, pernicious or virtuous, contrary to the commandments of God, or acts done for se only purpose to please oneself. There are both positive and virtuous human traditions. Those who do not conform to the commandments of God must be abandoned. The virtuous traditions, not conforming to the law of God, are like a foreign fire introduced into the holy place of God. We know what happened to Aaron's two sons, Nadab and Abihu, about the foreign fire illegally brought into the temple of God at its inauguration. They were consumed at the same time as the sacrifices. Yet they needed fire to consume the sacrifices of the Lord. Fire was a real need. But the provenance did not please God, hence the tragedy. So what is virtuous can be rejected if it does not conform to the pure law of God. Christians must be vigilant on the issue. Many Christians, coming from the animist traditions, are particularly concerned by this exhortation.

Be careful, having the tendencies of the Spirit does not mean that one will not commit a sin anymore. This means that in case of sin, quickly confess by invoking the blood of the Lamb – Jesus – to restore the communion with the Lord. The Lord knows this because, in the prayer taught to the disciples, He prescribed to pray **every day** *for the forgiveness of offenses as we forgive those who have offended us*. The Lord will lead His Christians on a path where they will triumph over sin. It is enough for them only to be ready for this sanctification, and the Lord will take care of everything. They need willpower and a dose of humility. Many Christians complain of their sins, but do not show any willingness to follow the Lord on the path of sanctification.

Finally, the Lord does not ask Christians to keep an accounting record of their acts of sanctification to know if they are eligible for the windows of heaven. They must continually address their prayers and supplications to the Lord without doubt, and their prayers will be answered at the right time.

Addressing all kinds of requests and supplications to God

> *«Praying always with all prayer and supplication in the Spirit, and **watching to this very thing with all perseverance** and supplication for all saints»* **Ephesians 6:18**.

This quotation from the Scripture denounces the poverty of the prayer life of many Christians. It insists however: *Watch with all perseverance*. One can dig the reason for a mediocre prayer life. Either the Christian does not believe that his prayer will reach the Lord, or he believes that a request sent once will suffice because, according to him, God has a memory. Either he believes that the problem can be solved outside prayer, or as he lives in a sort of desert, he thinks that there is no solution to his problem.

The Lord's message to Christians is: '**No matter what your eyes see and what your mind seizes in a poor and desolate environment, ask for the windows of heaven and you will see the glory of My Father'**. Let's not content with one request to God. God wants to hear us once, twice, three times, a hundred times, a thousand times. Let us not give up supplicating the Lord until we are completely satisfied.

The windows of heaven for young Nichols

This is the story of a young Christian named Nichols who, at the beginning of his faith, experienced the God who cares for His children, when He says:

> «*Therefore do not be anxious, saying, what shall we eat? Or, what shall we drink? Or, with what shall we be clothed? For the nations seek after all these things. For your heavenly Father knows that you have need of all these things. But* **seek first the kingdom of God and His righteousness; and all these things shall be added to you**. *Therefore do not be anxious about tomorrow; for tomorrow shall be anxious for its own things. Sufficient to the day is the evil of it*» (**Matthew 6:31-34**).

The young Nichols was experiencing salary arrears in a business plagued by cash flow difficulties, because of the global economic slump that seriously undermined his business sector.

One Sunday morning, a day of worship, he had only forty cents in his pocket. An amount that could barely buy him a poorly garnished sandwich. What could he do? The place of worship was seven kilometers away and the forty cents could not take him to his destination. But Nichols was one of those audacious Christians who keep their problems secret. According to the Bible that he had read, God asked His children not to worry about anything, but to enter a secret place to expose Him any need, because He sees and hears everywhere. Then he asked himself: will I skip the church for a money issue? Does God not deserve my entire life no matter what? He had made his mind: he was not going to skip the church for a last sandwich before death. Analyzing the distance to be covered, he decided to walk two kilometers, then to take a public transport for the remaining distance with the forty cents.

His overall plan was, once the church over, to rush back on a road with little traffic to avoid people noticing his hardship, to avoid also the compassion of other members of the church. He had difficulty showing ill-looking face. His status of son of God was his pride and he was not ready to compromise at all.

The outbound route went smoothly. The church took place. At the end, he put his plan into action. The return distance was approximately seven kilometers long.

After less than a kilometer by foot, he heard a vehicle honking behind him. The deserted street had made him understand that the horn was targeting him. Who could honk this Sunday, day of rest, on a deserted street? Turning around, he recognized the driver and stopped because Steve – his name – looked like he wanted to talk.

Hello Nichols, excuse me, would you grant me a moment? The invitation of Steve was serious. Yes, Nichols answered, serenely so as not to arouse suspicion of his hardship. Nichols sat in the vehicle, which, to his surprise, took the opposite direction of his house. Steve stayed another five kilometers away. Nichols armed himself with patience for the twelve kilometers he would have to deal with later. Nichols had faith and left everything at the Lord's hands.

Arrived at destination, Steve submitted to Nichols a project he had been designing for weeks. He knew that Nichols was working in the business sector dealing with projects of the like. Can you handle this file? Yes, Nichols answered. How long will it take you? A good week, Nichols replied, although he was able to complete the file in three or four days. But a week was usually the delay applied in this business. Steve went on: I planned two thousand dollars for the job. Does the amount suit you? Yes said Nichols. You need an advance payment, don't you? Yes M. Steve. Will one thousand and two hundred dollars suit you? Absolutely Sir. Then deal closed. Nichols received immediately one thousand and two hundred dollars in bank notes.

Leaving home with forty cents, barely enough to take him to the church, knowing that he would have to walk seven kilometers by foot and even twelve, Nichols found himself in the afternoon with a thousand and two hundred dollars, three thousand times its original asset.

God had just demonstrated that the windows of heaven are working twenty-four hours a day. Men have working days and hours. Aside from Israel (Saturday) and several Muslim countries

(Friday), Sunday is generally a non-working day in the rest of the world, the one where Nichols experienced the miracle. Nichols could have waited for Monday, the first working day of the week, but he trusted God who holds in his hands the windows of heaven.

The Heavenly Bank's assets for terrestrial Christians

Basic knowledge

> *«Do not lay up treasures on the earth for yourselves*, where moth and rust corrupt, and where thieves break through and steal. *But lay up treasures in heaven for yourselves*, where neither moth nor rust corrupt, and where thieves do not break through nor steal. For where your treasure is, there will your heart be also»* **Matthew 6:19-21**.

The bank is traditionally the place where one puts treasures in safety, sheltered from covetousness, destruction and theft. By asking Christians to privilege heavenly treasures over terrestrial ones, Jesus clearly invites His saints to credit their heavenly bank. He gives the reason: earthly treasures are not safe from *thieves, moth and rust*.

This statement is truth because it is enough to go around the world to know what has become of the immense riches of men and peoples of antiquity. In particular, what has become of the legendary riches of Solomon, King of Israel? Here is an estimate according to the Scripture:

«The weight of gold which came to Solomon in one year was six hundred sixty-six talents of gold (twenty tons), apart from the merchant men, and from the traffic of the traders, and from all the kings of Arabia, and from the governors of the lands. And King Solomon made two hundred targets of beaten gold; six hundred shekels of gold went into one target (six kilograms). And he made three hundred shields of beaten gold; three minas of gold went into one shield (one and half kilogram). And the king put them in the house of the forest of Lebanon. And the king made a great throne of ivory, and overlaid it with the best gold. The throne had six steps, and the top of the throne was round in the back part. And there were stays on either side on the place of the seat, and two lions stood beside the stays; and two lions were standing on the six steps, on this and on that side. There was not the like made in any kingdom. And all king Solomon's drinking vessels were of gold, and all the vessels of the house of the forest of Lebanon were of pure gold. None were of silver; it was counted nothing in the days of Solomon. For the king had at sea a navy of Tarshish with the navy of Hiram. Once in three years the navy of

> *Tarshish came bringing gold and silver, ivory, and apes, and peacocks. And King Solomon was greater than all the kings of the earth in riches and in wisdom»* (**1 Kings 10:14-23**).

To this day, there is no trace of this immense wealth, swept away by the episodes of a history rich in theft, moth and other sinister. What has become of the riches of the antic pagan temples, Greco-Roman temples and Egyptian pyramids? Looted.

This is what Jesus is talking about asking Christians not to amass riches on the earth. If the great riches of Solomon have not withstood the episodes of history, theirs will not resist. Jesus Christ asks His Christians to privilege the Heavenly Bank. It is clear that this Bank is perfectly managed by the Lord. If many terrestrial banks are well managed by men, the Celestial Bank will be greatly managed by the angels of God. This Bank is part of the windows of heaven that Christians can ask for when needed. The Celestial Bank has this advantage: it will never fall due to stock market crash or robbery. This Bank is safe, guaranteed by the Lord of glory in Whom Christians can fully trust.

Below, we give an overview of what the Heavenly Bank can do for men on the earth.

How do you hoard treasures in heaven?

> *«Jesus: **But lay up treasures in heaven for yourselves»** Matthew 6:20*

This question refers to daily financial exchanges. We all know how to hoard a treasure on the earth: it is stored in a secret place at home, at the public or private daycare, at the bank.

In asking that the treasures of His Christians are preferably amassed in heaven, while no one knows the visible stairway that connect to it, one can genuinely ask how this is possible.

The answer is given to us by the Scriptures: **It is by keeping the command of God that we hoard the treasures in heaven**. This is what Jesus says:

> *«Then the King (Jesus) shall say to those on His right hand, **come, blessed of My Father, inherit the kingdom prepared for you from the foundation of the world**. For I was hungry, and you gave Me food; I was thirsty, and you gave Me drink; I was a stranger, and you took Me in; I was naked, and you clothed Me; I was sick, and you visited Me; I was in prison, and you came to Me. Then the*

righteous shall answer Him, saying, Lord, when did we see You hungry, and fed You? Or thirsty, and gave You drink? When did we see You a stranger, and took You in? Or naked, and clothed You? Or when did we see You sick, or in prison, and came to You? And the King shall answer and say to them, truly I say to you, **inasmuch as you did it to one of the least of these My brothers, you have done it to Me»** (**Matthew 25:34-40**).

The above narration shows that the reward of God was given to the surprise of the beneficiaries, the righteous ones. Wanting to know more, these righteous were told: *inasmuch as you did it (good) to one of the least of these My brothers, you have done it to Me (Jesus).* It is the righteous ones who are content to obey God's command in favor of those in distress. Since these righteous had obeyed this command, they had amassed, without knowing it, a heavenly treasure that would at least profit them later, during the last judgment and the retribution of the righteous.

Scripture calls Christians never to stop doing good:

«We should not lose heart in well-doing, *for in due season we shall reap, if we do not faint»* (**Galatians 6:9**).

«You, brothers, **do not be weary in well doing»** (**2 Thessalonians 3:13**).

> «*Therefore to him who knows to do good, and does not do it, to him it is sin*» (**James 4:17**).

It is therefore in doing good relentlessly, that the Celestial Bank accounts will be credited under the supervision of the greatest Banker of all time, Jesus Christ, Almighty God.

Let us not confuse these treasures with the Christians' donations to Church. Voluntary donations reflect the Christians' gratitude to God for His blessings. Thus we honor God by sending voluntary donations to the Church. That does not count in the increase of the Celestial Bank account credit. It is as if we give God a royalty, a kind of tax. The goods that are piled up in heaven are acts that we do for our neighbor. A voluntary donation to the Church does not fall into this category, although the Church can allocate a portion of these donations to the poor. What is amassed in heaven therefore comes from acts of kindness in favor of the neighbor, unrelated to the donations to the Church. Christians must be careful not to think that their donations to the Church are acts of generosity towards people in distress. Jesus had already reprimanded the Jews for this mistake. He told them:

> «*And He (Jesus) said to them, **do you do well to set aside the commandment of God, so that you may keep your own tradition?** For Moses said, "honor your father and your mother." And, "whoever curses father or mother, let him die the death. But you say, if a man shall say to his father or mother, Corban! (that is, A gift to God, whatever you may profit by me) and*

> *you no longer allow him to do anything toward his father or mother, making the word of God of no effect through your tradition which you have delivered»* (**Mark 7:9-13**).

This passage from the Scriptures reflects how angry Jesus was with those who hid behind the donations to the temple for not honoring their parents.

The quotation **James 4:17** also warns Christians very clearly: *to him who knows to do good, and does not do it, to him it is sin.* Those who refuse to obey the commandments of the Lord, in matters of generosity, will expose themselves to the wrath of the Almighty. If we continue the narration of **Matthew 25** quoted above, we read the following:

> *«Then He (Jesus) also shall say to those on the left hand, **depart from Me, you cursed, into everlasting fire prepared for the devil and his angels.** For I was hungry, and you gave Me no food; I was thirsty, and you gave Me no drink; I was a stranger and you did not take Me in; I was naked, and you did not clothe Me; I was sick, and in prison, and you did not visit Me. Then they will also answer him, saying, Lord, when did we see You hungry, or thirsty, or a stranger, or naked, or sick, or in prison, and did not minister to You? Then He (Jesus) shall answer them, saying, truly I say to you, **inasmuch as you did not do it to one of the***

> *least of these, you did not do it to Me. And these (wicked) shall go away into everlasting punishment, but the righteous into everlasting life»* (**Matthew 25:41-46**).

Christians should not panic by the above narration, if they are in good heart. It is not a matter for them to keep an accounting register of their achievements and, in case of errors or omissions, to run everywhere to catch up. The Lord's response to errors is confession and repentance. Many Christians will certainly find themselves in a bad position in relation to the above. Far from this book the idea of arousing in them such anxiety. It is the Lord who acts in the Christians. It suffices for the Christian to be in good heart, and he will realize how the Lord works miracles by his arms. No pagan can obtain from the Lord that his heaven account be credited by doing humanitarian work on the earth. Many humanists even admit that God does not exist. This is the selfish search for the glory of men. But God does not give His glory to anyone. *For it is God who works in you both to will and to do of His good pleasure* (**Philippians 2:13**). The aim comes from God. The will and the doing also. So there is no personal glory to look for.

Perpetual sanctification is the best way for Christians to maintain loving dispositions favorable to the Lord's action. May they repent, through the blood of Jesus, in case of fault, and they may resume the normal course of their life as conquerors. Amen.

Nobody on the earth knows where the airport and planes are to take off towards the Celestial Bank. If we knew it, the rich and mackerel of this world would squat the place and anticipate the Christians. It is therefore by grace that God allows His Christians to amass treasures by doing good on the earth, with selflessness – *the left hand not knowing what the right hand does* – without waiting for the gratitude of the recipients.

The windows of Heaven and the retirement of Christians

Several advanced countries have succeeded in alleviating poverty and precariousness by creating a pension insurance system for people who are inactive because of their old age and disabilities. One can genuinely ask what will happen to retired Christians who have not made enough contributions for retirement and compensatory income. Many Christians living in less developed countries will worry about it.

For many years, this question had worried me. The Lord's answer had always been the same: *I am your retirement pension.* Many will recognize, especially those living in advanced countries, that it is difficult to experience this truth. How can one say to a Christian, beneficiary of a good retirement pension, that the Lord is his pension?

Yet the Lord's response did not change one iota. He is the retirement pension of the saints. They must not doubt it. By obeying the Lord's commandments in accordance with His vows – *seek My kingdom first and all the rest will be granted to you* – the saints will have no worries about their retirement. How can the Lord exhort not to worry about tomorrow and ignore the retirement of His Christians? It does not make sense. God is the retirement of Christians.

No matter whether our eyes see it or not, the Lord remains by far the retirement of the saints. Let us remember that many Bible heroes lived more than one hundred years despite a short working period: Abraham (175 years), Isaac (180 years), Jacob (147 years), Joseph (110 years), Moses (120 years), Job (around 150 years), Daniel (around 110 years), the apostle John (105 years). They lived for a long time while the pensioner protection system did not exist at all or did not match that of today.

How did they last so long, full of ages? Answer: God was their retirement. Christians in developed countries should not worry when their pension systems skid along with lower perceived pensions. Let them fix their eyes on the Lord, as the servant looks at the master's hand to hope for some providence.

It is important for older Christians in developed countries to stop thinking that they are entitled to substantial retirement, based on past social security contributions. That's the world. But the world passes as well as its idols. The retirement systems of this world, despite their usefulness, are mere idols. Christians who have contributed can benefit. But they must beware of showing the same bitterness and impatience as the pagans who have no Father God, for the Christian Father is faithful; He will not abandon them. Christians actually contribute to two pension funds: the terrestrial bank and the Celestial Bank of which it is said: *lay up treasures in heaven for yourselves* (**Matthew 6:20**).

When the earthly retirement system is running out of steam, the Celestial Bank comes to rescue. In fact, retired Christians are asked not to be satisfied with the earth fund. But also access to heavenly funds no matter he is too aged.

The Windows of heaven and the Christian getting aged

The words above, related to the retirement of Christians, can entirely apply in this chapter. There is more to say in addition to the income that seniors can expect from heaven.

With age growing, several functions of the human body lose their freshness, precursors signs of an end of life close to the *dust from which the man was drawn*. However, if the Scripture is without appeal on the return of the man to the dust, same saying for Christians, these must exploit thoroughly the complementary options of the grace of God.

asked to cover him up to the neck. He was definitely covered before sunshine. It was then that his disciples spread the news of his departure in abundant tears. Many Christians rushed to the scene and dug at the place of burial. The hole was dug and John's body was not found. John was then 105 years and 7 months old.

This example may well urge aged Christians not to resign themselves to a persistent illness because doctors say that it is normal for their age. They must fight the normality of this world, by all kinds of petitions addressed to the Lord of glory, until the Lord informs them that it is time to leave this world for a well-deserved rest. That's it, living on the earth with the windows of heaven and the Celestial Bank at your disposal.

The windows of heaven and the job of the saints

> «*Slaves, obey your masters according to the flesh, with fear and trembling, in singleness of your heart, **as to Christ**»* (**Ephesians 6:5**).

> «*Slaves, obey your masters according to the flesh in all things; not with eye-service, as men-pleasers, but in singleness of heart, **fearing God**»* (**Colossians 3:22**).

> «*Let as many slaves as are under the yoke count their own masters worthy of all honor,*

> *so that the name and doctrine of God may not be blasphemed*» (**1 Timothy 6:1**).

> «*Servants, be subject to your masters with all fear, not only to those good and forbearing, but also to the perverse ones*» (**1 Peter 2:18**).

> *God knows the saying that 'Whoever pays is the one who decides' (Humans).*

Have you ever wondered how Christians maintain their allegiance to the Lord while they are submitted to bosses of this world? Have we not often thought that the revenues from the Lord came from churches? How can the Lord maintain His authority over Christians if they are fed from other sources than Him?

Believe me, these questions are very important to the Lord. The Lord knows very well that a master who does not feed his slave – Christians are slaves to the Lord – is a fictitious master, and we are serious saying so. In fact, the Lord has already settled the question in these terms: *Whoever believes in Jesus no longer lives for himself, but for God.* The Scripture says indeed:

> «*Likewise count yourselves also to be truly dead to sin, but **alive to God through Jesus Christ our Lord**»* (**Romans 6:11**).

From there, the following conclusion: **Every Christian is a disciple subject to his ONLY Master Jesus Christ**. The masters of this world are only recipients to whom Jesus Christ assigns His disciple because every disciple is an ambassador of Christ (**2 Corinthians 5:20**).

Christians therefore no longer directly serve the masters according to the flesh. They serve Christ via these. The master's orders come from Christ. The salary of the Christian therefore comes from Christ through the master who can, according to the secret instructions of Christ, increase or lower that salary. The job done by the Christian is also directed to Christ via the master. The latter can approve but the Lord reject. The Lord can say that the master will accept a quality of 18/20, but He the Lord will require a 20/20 mark. To this end, the Christian must obey the Holy Spirit and redouble his efforts for a 20/20 performance, even if the master of the world is ready to be content with 18/20. Very often, the Lord will use the master of the world to criticize the work of the Christian, even if this work deserves 19/20. The master will say, for example: *Everything pleases me in what you have done, but there is something that troubles me. I am ready to pay you the job done, but I wish you would take this request into account.* Although very courteous, this opinion is nonetheless that of the Lord. It is up to the Christian to take it into account and everything will be perfect. The master will be happy and the Lord too.

It has happened that in a mission that I performed, all my partners appreciate the entire sheet except a column of numbers arousing curiosity. The Lord made me understand that this column was superfluous and I removed it. Result: no more comment but unanimous validation.

This is how the disciple of Jesus Christ can serve His Master everywhere, in all circumstances. *Whatever you do, do all to the glory of God»* (**1 Corinthians 10:31**).

Many poorly devoted Christians found themselves in the same way as pagan employees: dismissals, social changes, etc. These Christians followed the unbelievers in their strike movements. But the Lord may well ask His servant to work beyond the hours of service, without asking overtime payment. Simply because the Lord wants His servant to save a boss in trouble. He must follow the Lord instead of imitating unbelievers, many of whom believing that bosses are just thieves to fight by any means.

Christians must know that the services offered by them in their workplaces come from heaven and bear the mark of the kingdom of heaven. For the Christian *is no longer of the world*, but of the kingdom of heaven. As such, he may consider that the salary paid is not sufficient for the level and quality of the celestial services performed. Thus the salary paid by the bosses constitutes the earthly share, while the remainder, which should have taken into account the heavenly quality of service, is credited to the Christian in the Celestial Bank. Hallelujah! The Celestial Bank account credit of the

> Christian can help him in difficult situations: retirement, sickness, unemployment, unforeseen, etc. Let us suppose that the salary of a Christian, according to the boss of the world, is two thousand dollars, and that according to the heaven quality of service, his total salary is estimated at three thousand and five hundred dollars. The difference of one thousand and five hundred dollars, not paid by the boss according to the flesh, will be credited to this Christian's Celestial Bank account.

The accumulation of these heavenly credits will increase the Christian's treasures to heaven, as commanded by the Lord.

The Christian will therefore always be an employee of the Lord. The Lord may, as He pleases, make His servant available to the earthly boss. To begin with, here are the basic rules that this Christian must apply at his workplace:

- He has to work without flinching because he is under the hidden hierarchical authority of God. It is God who gives him His orders through the boss.
- He must be wary of strikes in general, especially those defying the authority of the boss. He must not be afraid of other strikers because his true Boss and Master is the Christ who has all power.

- He must not openly complain about his salary. If the boss does not intend to increase it, let the Christian wait patiently for the deliverance of the Lord. This deliverance always comes. If Sara waited for a child for years, despite the humiliation of being sterile, the Christian must also wait the necessary time before deliverance. When, despite the seriousness and discipline of the Christian, the boss of the world ignores his performance, a terrible judgment falls on him. Thus bosses were surprisingly replaced by Christians. This is how societies collapsed after the departure of Christians. Through these judgments, the Lord sends a message to the world to glorify and fear the heavenly Father. Egypt definitely lost its ancient glory after Moses freed the Hebrews from slavery. The slavery of Hebrew people on Egyptian soil made the glory of Egypt, which learned it at its expense. Egypt has not recovered its former glory.

- The Christian must not change his company according to the salary or mood of the boss. It is sad when a Christian quits a job because the boss is grumpy. It is the unbelievers who do this. The workplace of a Christian is chosen by the Lord according to precise criteria. Change of workplace or boss on a whim, as pagans do, can lead to the loss of faith in the Christian, which is perilous for his salvation. The Lord chooses a workplace taking into account the victorious battles that the Christian is going to take at this place.

- The Christian must not flinch because he works for the Lord who, at the opportune moment, will reward his efforts. The Christian might even ask to spend more time at his workplace. If the boss objects, for fear of overtime payment, that the Christian reassures him that he will ignore it. If the boss persists in his refusal despite the explanation, let this Christian continue this work outside the workplace. The boss will appreciate, will guess that his worker has spent overtime hours to solve the problem, and the Lord will reward him.

The windows of heaven and the managing organization of the church

Having already understood that the Lord links the life of His disciples to the providence of the heavenly windows, and not only to the very insufficient resources of the earth, then the managing organization of the churches can no longer go according to the world. The world only targets resources of the earth, while churches target the windows of heaven.

Church leaders must keep in mind that the windows of heaven will open to cover their earthly needs. To begin with, some financial management plan should be avoided. We want to say this: Systematically demanding that members contribute for a yes or no, this is not the faith that the Lord expects. Let us remember that to pay the tax of Caesar, Jesus had not solicited the earthly resources. He asked Peter to throw the hook into the water, which brought back enough to pay for Him and Peter. When it was question of feeding five thousand men, Jesus did not exploit the common box held at the time by Judas Iscariot – who stung in it – nor the group of sympathizers who followed Him. On the contrary, Jesus appealed to the windows of heaven, and the people could eat bread to satiety.

It is therefore understandable that some practice of puncturing the pockets of the members, according to the needs of the churches, is akin to harassment. The Lord does not like that.

Church leaders must always keep in mind that they have the windows of heaven at their disposal. They must pleasantly surprise the members by revealing to them how the Lord has miraculously solved an insurmountable issue. Christians must be serene knowing that their leaders are not greedy, ready to harass them for nothing. If leaders do not have faith, let them buy it from the Lord.

Imagine that Jesus was not stingy. Not at all. He was the incarnate generosity, expressed in most of the miracles He did. It is terrible to discover the fickleness of Christian leaders, coupled with astonishing greed. What a distressing sight when churches struggle with all their strength to hunt down the least money! They may think that they show the world how rigorous managers they are. No, in fact, they are stingy, worsen the opprobrium of the Lord of glory who was so generous.

Judas Iscariot stung in the earthly box while Jesus Christ moved with the windows of heaven always at His disposal. Judas was so blinded that he did not make the difference between the King of the Jews and thirty unfortunate pieces of silver. A sum that even its owners refused to recover. The difference is there. By dint of limiting their faith to earthly, insufficient and fragmented resources, church organizations have come to isolate themselves from each other. The difference between several church organizations is less a doctrinal divergence than a desire to protect their financial and material assets. If the churches were to look beyond earthly resources, by staring at the windows of heaven, as the Lord has asked, the boundaries between churches would be so derisory that they would disappear on their own. Alas, not only is this not the case, but the stinginess of churches opened the door to thieves. The world rumors about the crime of church officials in charge of financial affairs. Let's say no more.

Christians must not follow this very rigorous human model, apparently virtuous. Christians have access to the windows of heaven, not once but all time. Many Christians have been trained in some of the most prestigious management schools in the world. But what matters to the Lord is their ability, not to manage the earthly resources better than the pagans, but to seize the opportunities offered by the windows of heaven. If Jesus behaved like a human being riveted to the resources of the earth, He would have requisitioned all the bakeries around to feed thousands of people after a sermon that continued late into the evening. But it was not so. And for good reason! How can the general accounting system show that five loaves and two fish fed five thousand men? It is to this heavenly providence that the Lord calls His Christians who walk in faith and not by sight. In the presence of the Lord, heavenly management degrees are more valuable than terrestrial management degrees.

No matter how old a Christian may be, he must demand excellent health and not act like the world. The latter resign themselves to accept the inevitable as a fatality. Christians must not be fatalistic. As long as the Lord keeps them alive, they must demand a body in perfect health, in perfect working order. Scripture exhorts Christians to address all kinds of requests to the Father. Scripture did not set a limit, a ceiling in the scope of queries. Scripture mentions no exception for the elderly. No matter how old they are, Christians must ask the Lord for a body in good shape until He tells them, in a precise way, to prepare for departure, as Peter and Paul were divinely warned in their time.

> «**Peter** : *Knowing that the putting off of my tabernacle is soon, as indeed our lord Jesus Christ made clear to me*» (**2 Peter 1:14**).

> «**Paul** : *For I am already being poured out, and the time of my release is here*» (**2 Timothy 4:6**).

Without this clear and personal warning, the Christian must ask the Father for a body in good shape. He must insist on that.

Old age and departure of Apostle John. I cannot end this chapter without recalling how Apostle John left this world, 105 years old. Always in good health, the Lord told him that it was time to go. So he said goodbye and asked his disciples to dig a cross-shaped tomb in the sand. After hugging and comforting his disciples, he entered the tomb by himself and lay down there. He asked them to cover him to the knees. After a last farewell, he

The windows of heaven and the diseases of Christians

*«May the God of peace Himself sanctify you, and **may your whole spirit and soul and body be preserved blamelessly** at the coming of our Lord Jesus Christ»* **1 Thessalonians 5:23**.

*«And by the surpassing revelations, lest I be made haughty, a thorn in the flesh was given to me, a messenger of Satan to buffet me, lest I be made haughty. For this thing **I besought the Lord three times, that it might depart from me.** And He said to me, My grace is sufficient for you, for My power is made perfect in weakness. Most gladly therefore I will rather glory in my weaknesses, that the power of Christ may overshadow me»* **2 Corinthians 12:7-9**.

«But He (Jesus) was wounded for our transgressions; He was bruised for our iniquities; the chastisement of our peace was

> *on Him; and **with His stripes we ourselves are healed**»* **Isaiah 53:5.**

Jesus, our Lord, was in good health. Scripture does not mention any illness that He would have suffered. Jesus healed all the sick and disabled who were brought to Him, regardless of the severity of the illness or disability. He said that some diseases were the devil doing.

> *«And evening coming on, they brought to Jesus many who had been possessed with demons. And **He cast out the spirits with a word, and healed all who were sick**»* **(Matthew 8:14-16).**

Through this attitude of Jesus Christ during His visit to Peter's home, it appears that the state of sickness and disability is an anomaly in the kingdom of heaven of which Christians are members. On the other hand, the Church is immaculate, that is to say, without sin, without stains, wrinkles, or anything like that – so without disease.

Thus, a Christian is perfectly right in claiming a holy body, without disease or handicap. To maintain a state of illness or handicap, on the basis of the explanations of medicine, is either a bad teaching or a lack of faith. The Christian does not have to accept the illness, whatever the doctor may say. Rather he must insist on his healing.

In **2 Corinthians 12:7-8** above, the apostle Paul states about the physical suffering he had in the flesh: *Three times he besought the Lord that it might depart from him.* This is a firm demand of the servant of God in his right to have a holy and blameless body. This is the state of mind that the Lord expects of every Christian. The opposite would be an absence of faith in Christ, or simply paganism. A Christian who sticks to the rational explanations of medicine deceives himself. He should get out of this trap. The Christian must insist on the Lord until his illness or disability disappears. The windows of heaven are open to him for that. To him to claim his due – the health promised by the Lord.

In Paul's example, the Lord gives a reason for rejecting the apostle's request. On this basis, let us understand that only a precise and explained rejection of the Lord must allow the Christian to accept his fate. We insist that this message must be accurate and personal. The message of Jesus was addressed to Apostle Paul and only him; it was not a general exhortation to allow an illness or disability to flourish in the body of the Christian. The only reason for the Christian to accept the presence of an illness or disability must come from a clear, accurate and personal message from the Lord. He must not accept an exhortation to bear the disease from other Christians whose intention may be laudable but still carnal. These Christians do not suffer in their flesh; It is therefore easy for them to talk like the three witnesses gambling on Job's hardship. A Christian who suffers from illness and disability must insist on the

Lord for total and complete healing. It's his right up to total satisfaction.

The word of God is an effective way to achieve healing. According to **Isaiah 53:5** quoted above, Jesus carried on His cross all our diseases and handicaps, without exception. On this basis, the Christian must consider sickness or disability as a devil's scam and resist. Some diseases are clearly demons blowing the organ in pain. The Christian must oppose their pernicious actions, recalling his inheritance related to the condemnation of Jesus on the cross for the Christian's sake.

On the cross indeed, Jesus paid the ransom for all the faults and crimes of humanity (including the Christians); and the Father has approved this ransom. Jesus having already undergone the condemnation of the Christian on His cross, the latter must loudly recall this heritage – the demons concerned will hear because they are not deaf. That is to say, the Christian does not have to undergo another condemnation in addition to the cross that Jesus suffered; and the demons will go away because the double condemnation is not legal. He can pray by putting his hand on the organ in pain so that the demons feel personally concerned; and the inheritance of the cross of Jesus will be given to this Christian. If the organ seems recalcitrant despite prayer, an anointing of oil (even a fast) will be necessary – when laying hand – to overcome the disease. Jesus has conquered the world, as well as the demons and diseases that the latter can cause.

«And when He (Jesus) had called to Him His twelve disciples, He gave them **authority over unclean spirits, to cast them out, and to heal all kinds of sickness and all kinds of disease»** (**Matthew 10:1**).

«And as you go, proclaim, saying, the kingdom of heaven is at hand. **Heal the sick, cleanse the lepers, raise the dead, cast out demons.** *You have received freely, freely give»* (**Matthew 10:7-8**).

We say Amen!

Read the Scriptures to appropriate the heavenly and earthly heritage of Christians

Being the sword of the Spirit, the word of God is a powerful energizer of the Christian life

«*Take the helmet of salvation, and* **the sword of the Spirit, which is the word of God**» **Ephesians 6:17**.

«*And these words which I command you this day* **shall be in your heart**. *And you shall carefully teach them to your sons, and shall talk of them when you sit in your house and when you walk by the way, and when you lie down, and when you rise up.* **And you shall bind them for a sign upon your hand, and they shall be as frontlets between your eyes. And you shall write them upon the posts of your house, and on your gates**» **Deuteronomy 6:6-9**.

The Holy Spirit will not be effective in the life of a Christian who does not devour the Scriptures. It's like a car without fuel. The car will not move. It's like a tuneless phone set. It won't ring. Two key words deserve our attention: (i) the soul of man has a penchant for rebellion. That is to say, without a binding discipline, a Christian should not expect his soul to encourage him to read the Scriptures; (ii) without knowledge of Scriptures, the Holy Spirit will lack fuel to function properly in the Christian. A Christian can perfectly feel the inner touch of the Spirit – ointment – but without the help of Scriptures, it will be hard to stick an understanding to that feeling.

As recalled in **Deuteronomy 6:6-9** above, the Christian is invited to devour the Scriptures, to fill his life with them. Thus the Holy Spirit will always put a word of knowledge and wisdom in the mind of the Christian, on every occasion favorable or not. The prophet had promised that God would inscribe His Law on the hearts and no longer on the stone tablets of Mount Sinai. It is the Holy Spirit, present in the spirit of the Christian, who represents this Law. Scripture explicitly states that the Spirit of the Lord is also a Law: *The law of the Spirit of life* in Jesus-Christ (**Romans 8:2**). It is this Law that will react in the life circumstances of the Christian. Provided that the Christian binds his life on the Holy Scriptures.

It will happen very often that the Christian feels an inner touch – ointment – without being able to stick a meaning to this touch. It is little by little that the Spirit will fix the Christian's intelligence on specific Scriptures recorded in his memory. But if the Christian does not know these Scriptures, he will stick only to the perceived touch, nothing more, which could be disabling. This Christian sees but cannot explain. He does not help many others.

Let's suppose the Lord does not approve a preaching. The irritation will evidently grow in the Christian's spirit – seat of the Holy Spirit. But without knowledge of Scriptures, he will not be able to disassemble the preacher's errors. Let us remember the temptation of Jesus by the devil. The devil quoted Scripture verses to manipulate the Lord. But the Lord also invoked Scriptures to counter the devil. It is not enough to be irritated in one's mind because of a pernicious preaching, it must be dismantled point by point to be relieved. The drama is that the sermons are always recorded in the memory of the listener. These sermons return in a loop in the memory of the Christian. If these sermons are of the Lord, the Christian will take benefit. Otherwise, he will be confused. But how will the Christian dismount a pernicious preaching if he knows very little about Scriptures? As Jesus did against the tempter, only memorized scriptures will constitute a solid bulwark against such manipulations.

Forcing our soul to read the Scriptures

Let us not forget that it is in our human spirit – not in the soul – that the Holy Spirit sits at the instant you become a Christian. The soul of the Christian is not the seat of the Holy Spirit. Like intelligence and will, the soul is subject to change. King David already summoned his soul to praise the Lord. Here are some excerpts regarding this illustrious hero:

> *«**My soul shall make its boast** in Jehovah»* (**Psalms 34:2**).

> *«Why are you cast down, O **my soul**, and moan within me? **Hope in God**; for I shall praise Him for the salvation of His face»* (**Psalms 42:5**).

> *«**Wake up, my soul**! Wake up, harp and lyre! I will awake the dawn»* (**Psalms 57:8**).

> *«**My soul, be silent only to God**; for my hope is from Him»* (**Psalms 62:5**).

> *«**Bless Jehovah, O my soul**, and forget not all His benefits»* (**Psalms 103:2**).

> *«Praise Jehovah. **Praise Jehovah, O my soul**»* (***Psalms 146:1***).

By these words, the Christian is invited not to yield to laziness or to the rebelliousness of the soul. For example, our body particularly enjoys staying in bed in the morning, warm under a thick blanket. The Christian must then summon his soul to stand up and thank God before starting the day.

Many Christians think that by submitting to the soul, they will perceive the Holy Spirit's will, which they assimilate to those moments when the soul aspires to meet God. It happens to the soul to feel the desire for spirituality, despite its general tendency to rebellion. But if the Christian sticks to this free will, he will see his spiritual life going down.

How to read the Bible? The best way to read the Scriptures, despite their thick volume, is just to read them. It is recommended to follow a discipline according to each one disposition. On a personal basis, we recommend that every day a Christian reads one or two chapters, taking care to mark the end of the last chapter to avoid re-reading and omissions. Once started, a chapter must absolutely be finished because the beginning of a chapter recalls the context of the narration to grasp all the nuances. It is not recommended to stop at mid-chapter. In this case, next time you will have to restart the whole chapter. I usually read until the page is turned – for a paperback Bible. This is my discipline: the end of the chapter, after turning the page, is a good indicator to pause. So next day, my reading will begin at the page marker. Thanks to this discipline, I hardly make mistake on the chapters already read and those to be read; and the whole Bible is devoured in two years. Then a new cycle starts again. This is also the reason why we suggest to read the Bible from Genesis to Revelation, in that order. If a Christian reads everyday chapters on a random basis, he will not be able to maintain a rigorous discipline, let alone telling in which level of reading he is – start, middle or end of Bible. The above strategy needs to be adjusted in case of an electronic Bible.

The wrong method is to devour many chapters in a row, especially during holidays, as it will be difficult to replicate this performance on a consistent basis. Then one will state that the Bible is a hard-to-read book. Then one will postpone the next reading. But reading small quantities according to the above planning, guarantees the Christian continual spiritual nourishment to the satisfaction of the Lord. He will then see his reading become more effective, he will have permanent talks with the Lord, kind of rich supper.

Swallow the daily milk of the Word of God. We insist that it is necessary to read the Scriptures bit by bit as the daily milk before starting the day. We recommend that there is no interruption of more than one day. Usually, at the end of a book, I give myself one day break before moving to the next book – 66 books in a common Bible. We recommend that you do not allow more than one day off unless special circumstances. The problem is that it is difficult to re-motivate one soul after a long pause, because bad habits take over. Two or three days break are not fatal, but bad habits having hard skin, it is better to shorten the pause so that it does not extend indefinitely. It is also a bad idea to delay Scripture reading until summer vacation. It's like depriving a baby of his daily milk, thinking that he will have plenty of time on the weekend. The growth of the baby will be slowed down. As will be slowed the progress of the Christian who does not maintain a constant discipline in Bible reading.

Protect his reading from devil's disturbances. The moment of reading the Scriptures is dreaded and disturbed by the devil. So we advise Christians to protect their readings to avoid the many disturbances of which the enemy has the secret: drowsiness, fatigue, sudden priorities, etc. The enemy knows how to provoke seemingly legitimate needs when the Lord's moment arrives: the crying baby, a telephone call, an urgent need in and out. Protection is done by asking the Lord to cover with the blood of Jesus the time and place chosen to read and pray, to ward off all the attacks of the devil during reading and praying. May the Lord protect your thoughts against negative and positive distractions. If the enemy knows how to hide behind legitimate needs, God is above circumstances legitimate or not. The most favorable time for reading is around six in the morning at waking. This moment can be slightly delayed on weekends and days off.

Usefulness of other Christian books. What about other books published by Christians? Can one maintain a reading of Scriptures alongside reading other religious books? The works of the saints contribute to the spiritual nourishment of the Christian, since these works regularly rely on Scriptures. These works therefore maintain the spiritual milk the Christian needs daily. However, if in parallel with the reading of other religious books, the Christian maintains a lite reading of Scriptures such as, for example, a chapter every two days, instead of a chapter every day, then it will be perfect, one does not exclude the other.

God takes pleasure when His child goes in His Word. God is always delighted when His children discover the Scriptures to stick on. God will therefore bring complete joy to those who make it their habit and put His Word in practice as explained below. So it is noticed that whoever likes reading will read more; not only the Bible, but also other books inspired by God. While one who does not read the scriptures will increasingly have hard time reading them. This is the lesson taught by the Lord: *To him who possesses, it will be added to infinity; but to him who misses it, even the little he possesses will be taken away.* We must therefore take good habits and not let anything go. The more you love the Scriptures, the more God will reveal to you the nuances and diamonds that are hidden there. The process is long but profitable in terms of spiritual and material blessings. It's about creating your own addiction to the Word. Such an addiction is more auspicious than other addictions of life.

Living proof. My personal case can serve as an illustration of the above. You will see for yourself, through this book and many others in my collection, how much I am immersed in the Scriptures. When the Holy Spirit makes a chapter necessary, Bible verses flow as I pass on the message of the Lord. As soon as a verse comes to mind, I take care to check the source so as not to miss anything, using the most popular versions of the Bible. Why? Because they are buried in me for more than thirty years of meeting with the Lord of glory. Some will argue that the human brain is very skilled. One thing is certain, to date, science has not been able to establish any limit to the human brain. However, if it was about brain genius, I would have never believed. Just figure out that when a Bible verse always arrives at the right time – among hundred-and-fifty-thousand verses – to face a threat or confirm a truth, that it is always the day a collaborator defaulted, that suddenly it comes to you to read more deeply his report and to detect the blunder, and this happens hundreds of times, it is difficult for you to put these coincidences on the stroke of luck, unless chance is as powerful as God. No, it is the work of the Holy Spirit among Christians following the path Jesus Christ set in His time. The desire to read the Bible is probably due to the fact that I am at beginning a scientist, and for the sake of scientist way, we like to check more by ourselves than to copy from third parties, even though these are useful to the body of Christ. We do not need to be scientist to have this approach. The fear of being insidiously manipulated by the most educated was also my motivation. By drowning in Scripture at the beginning of my faith, I was able to wrap myself with the Word as a filter for all the words and advices I received, regardless of personality: brother and sister in Christ, pastor, veteran, deacon, prophet, spiritual guide, elder, etc. I used to relaunch an interlocutor by mentioning very precisely a verse related to the topic of discussion, to make sure nothing was misunderstood from a verse, and to know the feeling of my interlocutor on such command of the Lord. Believe me, by this discipline, I was able to find my way out of many difficult situations, along with refreshing the memory of many. This discipline has also been used in my relations with the non-Christian world, especially the business world. This is to avoid sinning or irritating God like those Christians who are faithful on Sundays but faithless the other days where they behave like pagans. If you find it difficult to read one or two chapters a day, read in just the bearable amount such as one or two paragraphs, while making sure to indicate the end of reading for a quick recovery that will save you boring repetitions. And the Bible will be completely devoured too. The Lord has not indicated a volume of daily reading. This is just a proposal from an experienced person with no desire to impose anything. But the Lord exhorts to watch and pray, which necessarily comprises the reading of His Word. Come on dear reader! You will get there like that illiterate widow whose story is related below.

Do you know an ancient book that we continue to devour with appetite two thousand years after its publication? The Bible is that book. This indicates that the Bible is the book of the immutable truth of God. Old books have been abandoned because their contents have not passed the trial over centuries; scientific discoveries making these books obsolete. The Christian can therefore trust the revelations of the Bible.

He who does not devour the Holy Scriptures is like an employee who ignores the rights and obligations he is bind to. He is likely to be told by the judge that he has crossed the line, that he does not meet the conditions for the claimed compensation.

He who does not devour the Holy Scriptures is also like an heir who does not know the heritage he is entitled to, a legacy defined in the testament which he does not want to read.

He who does not devour the Holy Scriptures is still like one who lets himself be struck and stepped on. He takes blows that he should not. He does not know whether he should be hit or not, where the blows should come from, whether the blows he should land are allowed or not.

He who devours the Holy Scriptures is rather a wise man who knows, understands and anticipates everything to the glory of God the Father.

Story of an illiterate widow who read the Bible

Fifteen years ago, I visited an old woman in her sixties, whom I knew to have not gone beyond class one of elementary education. The story is that her late husband, himself low educated, ended the learning program his wife was following because one day she got a good mark at a test. The man was afraid that his wife would embrace an exciting career at the expense of him, a rather modest husband.

As a widow, she really was illiterate. She could mumble as possible familiar language coming from radio and hearsay.

What caught my attention during my visit was the big Bible opened on her table, a Bible taken from her late husband's affairs. Knowing she was illiterate, I showed her my surprise. She understood and informed me that she was reading the Bible well. I exclaimed then: How do you, who have not passed class one of elementary school? Her answer was that she had always been curious to know what the old Bible found in her husband's affairs could contain, a husband she had never seen reading the Bible, as far as she could remember. She told that when her husband had prevented her from taking the course mentioned above, she had already learned the basics of ABC. Thus, by combining this method with radio listening and hearsay, she was able to identify the words of the Bible and their meaning.

I was amazed by what I was watching: an elderly woman, illiterate, widow, who from rudimentary materials, had managed to forge her way to the Word of God, the sword of the Spirit. Hallelujah!

With that, I realized that at the end of time, this widow will rise up to judge those who had several excuses not to read the Scriptures. What could be the strength behind this desire to discover the Holy Scriptures? Determination. She wanted to know what God said to the men and women of this world. And she succeeded.

There is therefore no excuse for those who do not read the Scriptures.

The Bible: the only rule of the Christian life

Someone might also say that the Bible is the contract between a Testator (God) and His joint-heirs (Christians). This may surprise at first. How can the Bible govern the life of the Christian in a law-regulated city like the one we live in? This is a main concern.

The answer comes from Jesus who, by saying *Let the dead bury their dead,* implied that the national laws were intended for the dead – pagans. Then what! Is Jesus wrong when He says pagans are dead? Do Scriptures not indicate that Christians are alive and pagans dead? No offense! Christians are alive and pagans dead. Jesus is not ashamed of His words, even if they are hard at times. Do the abominations and the continual decadence of the earth not suggest such words? Are we at the end of our surprises on the propensity of this earth to generate abomination in defiance of the Word of God who created it?

He who is sincere will recognize that, dealing with the requirements of God's holiness transcribed in the Scriptures, the laws of the earth are rather lax. He who honors the law of God will be far above the morals of this world, so perfect is the law of God. When Jesus was on the earth, He was simply blameless. It was by Jealousy that Pharisees and priests found default in Him by asserting, for example, that He was doing His miracles for Satan's sake. Many peoples, even soldiers of the occupying Roman army, came to beg Jesus for miracles. Every Christian who regularly observes the command of God will see that no law of the earth can resist him when it comes to morality. In fact the Christian's life will be so holy that pagans will have to choose between begging him to reveal the God he serves or hating him out of sheer jealousy – the second option is usually chosen in this decadent world.

Does that not make the Christian a handsome man? Absolutely. The Christian is handsome because he keeps the command of God. Pagans are ugly because first they are dead, second they do not keep the command of God, and they are even incapable of it because it is by the help of the Holy Spirit – whom pagans do not have – that Christians obey God.

The Christian with all parts of his life is therefore invited to comply with the Holy Scriptures without fail. Then he will see the glory of God on a regular basis. His house will be really built on a rock: *The rain came down, and the floods came, and the winds blew and beat on that house. And it did not fall, for it was founded on a rock.* (**Matthew 7:25**).

Terrestrial inheritance: the Christian's rest

The Christian, his physical appearance and the eyes of others

The Christian lives in the same body as an ordinary human being. He can be taken for anyone. As human being, every Christian cares about his appearance. Even a Christian woman cares on how she affects those around her. What woman, in general, does not look around her to know, from people staring, if her outfit suits her well?

That everyone is reassured. By making the Christian His ambassador on the earth, the Lord has settled all these questions. From now on, Christians must be aware that, no matter how much care they put on their appearance, **the impression they will make on people outside is what Jesus has decided**. For example, if a Christian woman puts all her efforts to appear beautiful, the Lord may pass her off as someone else; and too bad for the expenses. It is the same with brethren in Christ. It is sad that a Christian, anxious to have an advantageous appearance, considers, like pagans, plastic surgery to highlight such part of his body.

The Christian must praise the Lord for how he looks like. God is not ashamed of the work of His hands. The Lord did not say that we will judge angels only if we are more beautiful than them. Surely, angels will always be more beautiful than men, whatever the plastic surgery undergone by the latter.

Many testimonies of Christians establish that God can change the way they look like, either in a definitive way, or in a context that requires the Christian to be regarded as someone else. One day, I was questioned by my boss who wondered if I had the complexion X – more favored in the city I lived in. To my negative answer, he added: Why this office's secretary that we met together yesterday asks me how is your friend with complexion X? Knowing that I was the person concerned, my boss was very surprised – me too – because he was jealous that such an honor be granted to me. I was really embarrassed by this case because my boss liked to be valued more than all his employees. But the Lord let me know that He was behind all that. I do not count opportunities in life where I have been taken for someone else, most often to my great advantage. Glory to God who can, according to the context, advantageously modify the way His children look like.

The Christian must therefore rest in God for all that touches his physical body. That he does not getting nightmares, as pagans do, on the different ways to enhance his look. Such worries have led many people into a dead end: failed plastic surgery, irreversibly ruinous makeup for the body and health. The Lord has delivered us. Glory to God! This is not a call to neglect our body. A Christian must have a proper dress without negligence. But he must also feel free and relaxed, without maintaining the unhealthy complexes because of the eyes of others. On the question of clothing, Jesus says this in particular:

> *«**And why are you anxious about clothing?** Consider the lilies of the field, how they grow. They do not toil, nor do they spin, but I say to you that even Solomon in his glory was not arrayed like one of these. Therefore if God so clothes the grass of the field, which today is, and tomorrow is thrown into the oven, **will he not much rather clothe you, little-faiths?**»* (**Matthew 6:28-30**).

Let the Christian relax therefore in regard to his appearance, his dress in particular, and the eyes of others. The Lord takes care of everything, beyond what the Christian can hope for.

The Christian must bear the opprobrium of Christ

> *«Therefore let us go forth to Him (Jesus) outside the camp, **bearing His reproach (opprobrium)**»* **Hebrews 13:13**.

> *«He who loves father or mother more than Me is not worthy of Me. And he who loves son or*

*daughter more than Me is not worthy of Me. And **he who does not take up his cross and follow Me is not worthy of Me**»* **Matthew 10:37-38**.

*«So then, **everyone of you who does not forsake all his possessions**, he cannot be My disciple»* **Luke 14:33**.

Alas many Christians behave as enemies of the cross of Christ. How can a Christian behave as an enemy of the cross of Christ? In addition to the sins he can commit, there is the rejection of Christ's opprobrium.

As the Scriptures above state, Christians must be prepared to bear the reproach of Christ. The dictionary defines opprobrium as a big humiliation. Those who have never been humiliated in their lives will have to get used to it. It is an obligatory passage for all the sheep of the Lord, so that nothing else counts outside the will of God. Jesus Himself suffered humiliation. The Christian *being no greater than his Master*, he must prepare to be humiliated in his turn. This is what the Scriptures affirm. There is no way out.

Being a Christian is a message sent to the world saying: *Hate me if you care! Because I am no longer with you.*

Jesus invites His Christians to be ready to:

- Hate father, mother, wife, children, brothers and sisters, and even their own lives because of Him.
- Carry their cross and follow Him.
- Give up everything they have for Him.

No derogation is possible. Jesus wants a total surrender of the Christian. This is the place to note that there are many situations in which the Christian may be confronted with the opprobrium of Christ.

- To take the side of the strong without checking whether this camp militates for the truth and the justice, it is to reject the reproach of Christ.
- To sign a document because the majority has signed it, or because one does not want to suffer nor to be persecuted by this majority – example: to lose one's job – also falls under the forfeiture with regard to Christ who, Him, will be ashamed of this Christian before His Father.
- To blindly support one's child, despite his obvious faults, is to love one's child more than the Lord.
- To blindly support the position of his clan, his family, his country, while they are wrong and guilty, also falls under the contempt of the cross of Christ.
- Refusing to turn the second cheek, to give up the second tunic and to travel an additional kilometer when under duress also amounts to rejecting the opprobrium of Christ.

There are several comparable situations in which Christians are called to bear the reproach of Christ. In reality, it's not easy, so not at all. Let us remember Peter openly denying the Lord before His jailers. It is to say to what point, to carry the opprobrium of Christ is not easy. Peter repented and became the one we know, braving openly the Jewish Council of Jerusalem which, a couple of weeks earlier, had sentenced Jesus to death.

I like to recall a very apt hymn about the reproach of Christ. Here is a short excerpt:

> *But **the path of Calvary**
> Is **narrow and perilous**.
> It's **a lonely way**,
> **Hard and dark**.*

Christians must not be mistaken about what awaits them. To promise them mountains and wonders during their earthly pilgrimage has nothing to do with the gospel of Christ. Many Christians are so eager to fill their churches that they preach a gospel at a discount and get a confession of the lips. Christians, resulting from this process, are often the adventurers of the Church. They are the ones who hear the word on a stony ground. Hardly the sun appeared, the word dry because not having found the good ground.

Let us not forget that Jesus Christ had to endure the rejection of His own biological family. His family, incredulous like the majority of the Jews, let him know that it was in Jerusalem that a prophet was to prove himself, and not in Galilee, where Jesus had just performed his first miracles.

Far be it from us to minimize the suffering and loneliness of many Christians because of their faith. The rejection of his own, of his own mother for example, is not easy to face with. However, it is the cross to wear. Jesus did not say that it would be easy to endure. The Christian is invited to persevere despite the pain. His reward will be great even before the Lord's arrival. In case of error, we have, like the apostle Peter, the opportunity to repent and go forward, bearing the reproach of Christ to the glory of God the Father.

The opprobrium consolidates the faith of the Christian. It goes without saying that the opprobrium of Christ puts the Christian in a critical position where he feels alone in the face of adversity. The Christian suffers from loneliness when he has to oppose everyone – including relatives and friends – in the name of Christ. It's not that he's unaware of the situation. He is fully aware that he is taking a minority position, which can lead to charges of arrogance. But he must stay firm because that is what the Lord commands him. This is what the Lord did when, hunted by the Jews, He made a clear resolution to go to Jerusalem. This is what Paul did when he hastened to Jerusalem as prophecies announced his arrest. The shame is not a friend, but it helps to live critical situations that only Christians, determined and consecrated, can live. It is in these moments that the Holy Spirit, the Comforter, redoubles tenderness and consolation to maintain the Christian in a positive dynamic. He will come out of this ordeal with unshakeable faith.

The opprobrium allows for occasional and frank rewards. No worker works without pay. The reproach of Christ is a productive investment that yields. Jesus says about it:

> «*And Jesus answered and said, truly I say to you, there is no man that has left house or brothers or sisters or father or mother or wife or children or lands for My sake and the gospel's sake, **but he shall receive a hundredfold now in this time, houses and brothers and sisters and mothers and children and lands with persecutions**, and in the world to come, eternal life*» (**Mark 10:29-30**).

Note the precision: '***now in this time***' that is to say that the Christian is not obliged to wait for the return of Jesus Christ to pick up the dividends of his labor. It can be painful to remember the ancient heroes who waited a long time, sometimes even too much to the taste of today, before getting what they hoped for. This is the case of Sara who waited her ninetieth year to give birth to the heir of Abraham, her husband. Rebecca waited twenty years, Rachel about twelve years, Anne – mother of the prophet Samuel – certainly more, while Elizabeth gave birth to the prophet John the Baptist in her old age. Although Scripture does not explicitly exclude such delays in these end times, it is possible that the post-centennial life expectancy of the inhabitants of antiquity is the reason for this. Sara died at the age of one hundred and twenty-seven, while women's life expectancy today rarely exceeds eighty in developed countries. We do not know how long Job's ordeal lasted, but it ended one day, to the glory of God.

The experience of many faithful Christians testifies that the Lord multiplies the opportunities of relaxation and consolation among His Christians to, at the same time, consolidate their faith and reward their perseverance. It is not easy to preach the gospel to a swarm of witnesses when one is constantly in a situation of precariousness and vulnerability. God makes His children triumph in the world, against their enemies in particular, long before the announced return of Christ. It's a certainty.

The opprobrium makes it possible to unite with the spirits of the authors of the Bible. This does not show in appearance, but we must not be mistaken about the situation experienced, in their time, by the saints of the Holy Scriptures: Matthew, Mark, Luke, John, Paul, Peter, James, Jude, etc. Seeing several church systems holding worship in high places, rich in ancient carvings and high-priced canvases, may suggest that the Scriptures were written in favorable conditions. This is not true. Just as Jesus found the bleaching of the graves of dead martyred prophets hypocritical; for the whiteness of these sepulchres falsely suggested that these prophets had died of a sweet death. Paul wrote most of his epistles behind bars. Others were regularly on the run, hunted by the enemies of the truth, hidden by Christians braving the anti-Christian royal edicts. The opprobrium allows the Christian to enter into the shoes of these heroes of the faith to better understand the context in which the Scriptures were written and propagated. Needless to say how much those who bear the reproach of Christ are open-minded to understand the Scriptures in their diversity.

Terrestrial inheritance: the children of God are FREE

I do not know anyone on the earth who can claim the freedom Jesus took during His earthly journey: He interrupted the storm, marched on the water, turned the water into wine, raised the dead, delivered the possessed, multiplied the bread, yielded neither to King Herod nor to the lax and corrupt Jewish clergy. Nothing resisted him in fact. He was free, really free. He said:

> *«Therefore if the Son shall make you free, you shall be free indeed»* (**John 8:36**).

Freed from the prejudices of the world

Skin, nationality, gender, culture, birth place, diploma, job and housing are cause of many prejudices. How many times have you suffered from being of low birth, low nationality, low facies? Yet you were aware of being up to the challenge. But unfortunately, something out of your control appeared and you were demoted. The Christian must reassure himself: Jesus Christ triumphed over the world and all its prejudices. He says indeed:

> *«In the world you (Christians) shall have tribulation, but be of good cheer. **I have overcome the world**»* (**John 16:33**).

Which diploma did Joseph have, the Hebrew, promoted number two of ancient Egypt, then as dominant as the United States today? Yet Egypt did not lack eminent academicians who could ensure the mission of Joseph. Have they not invented the famous pyramids that have survived to this day, with their mummies, three thousand five hundred years after their construction? Joseph had no formal education since he had been a slave and a prisoner. The Hebrews of the time were considered a caste of untouchables since the Egyptians hated eating with them (**Genesis 43:32**). The story says however that Joseph did not only save Egypt from a great disaster, but also a seventy-people-family, the seed of Israel nation today.

What diploma did Daniel have, one of the Jewish deportees in Babylon? He had no formal diploma in a foreign city that would not have recognized his resume in any case. Yet by his genius, Daniel became the third VIP (very important personality) of the most powerful state of the world at the time, under several successive monarchs.

Many other cases can be recalled such as David slaying the giant Goliath while still a teenager (without warrior skills, he killed Goliath with the slingshot and the stone); such as Rahab, a former prostitute in Jericho, who became the ancestor of King David and Jesus Christ. All these examples should reassure Christians of their status: They do not have to fear not having the same pedigree as those of the world. They are special. They have a diploma that the world does not have: the Holy Spirit.

Freed from the tyranny of good manners and fashion effects

We must recognize that good manners are also sources of prejudices and discriminations in this world. Thus the populations of the big cities consider those of the other cities as barbarians, wild, ignorant, rough and manner-less. Jesus Himself was accused of being from a gloomy city of Nazareth in Galilee, of eating with tax collectors, of not washing hands before meals. All these good manners are pretty to see. At a time when absolute monarchies dominated the world, each social class was distinguished by a dress code in addition to bodily gestures of courtesy. But for the Lord, these rituals and good manners are not primordial anymore. Christians are called to free themselves from their tyranny. Do you eat at times not indicated by human tradition? No problem. Do you want to celebrate God apart from the consecrated days of worship? Feel free. Do you want to eat meat when the vegetarian diet is de rigueur? Feel free. Have you been told that you need to apply a precautionary measure before you commit? Go for it! The Lord will be with you. *Where the Spirit of the Lord is, there is freedom.* Have you been told that such food is favorable or unfavorable in this context? Let be guided by the Spirit and not by good manners. You are first of all the crown princes of the kingdom of heaven. Apostle Paul had already rebelled against the tyranny of these traditions. He said for example:

> *«But now, knowing God, but rather are known by God, **how do you turn again to the weak and beggarly elements to which you again desire to slave anew? You observe days and months and times and years**. I fear for you, lest somehow I have labored among you in vain. Brothers, I beseech you, be as I am; for I am as you»* (**Galatians 4:9-12**).

Sometimes, good manners have the unacknowledged purpose of subjugating docile and fragile people. It is a shame to find these shameful doings in the Church of Jesus Christ. Apostle Paul rebelled against these methods in harsh terms as follows:

> *«**For you endure if anyone enslaves you, if anyone devours, if anyone takes from you, if anyone exalts himself, if anyone strikes you in the face**. I speak according to dishonor»* (**2 Corinthians 11:20-21**).

Christians are free because Jesus has set them truly free. Amen.

Freed from the barriers of science

As citizens of the kingdom of heaven, Christians should not be surprised to experience situations rarely mentioned in the world.

Good or bad inextricable situations will happen to them. The kingdom of heavens being different from the earth, Christians should not be surprised that the laws of science could often not prevail where they live. By multiplying bread, turning water into wine, walking on water, Jesus showed that the laws of science are pointless compared to the kingdom of heavens. That is, the laws of science could lose their effects on Christians.

In interrupting the storm, Jesus was also showing that He was more competent than all the weather stations on the earth. The latter can at best predict a storm, but we have never heard that a weather station had interrupted a storm like Jesus did.

Christians must not lock themselves into human boundaries of knowledge. Let them stop suffering because the Lord is above science.

Freed from the worship of holy days, holy places and holy meals

The man is naturally inclined towards religion. Many believe that this tendency is to fill the void left in the spirit of our ancestors Adam and Eve after the Fall. It is however a reality that the human being tends to develop a religious activity. He is superstitious. This explains why, despite the call of Jesus and His disciples not to erect holy days, places and meals, Christians persist in doing so. Let's see what Jesus said in His time:

> «*The hour is coming when you shall neither worship the Father in this mountain nor yet at Jerusalem. (...) But the hour is coming, and now is, when* **the true worshipers shall worship the Father in spirit and truth***, for the Father seeks such to worship Him. God is a spirit, and they who worship Him must worship in spirit and in truth*» (**John 4:21-24**).

According to the Law of Moses, every Jew had to pray the face turned towards the holy city of Jerusalem. Commemorations under the Law could only be done in Jerusalem. Therefore, these solemnities were occasions for regrouping Jews from diaspora in Jerusalem. In addition to the holy place of Jerusalem, the days of the said commemorations were also holy days.

But Jesus came to announce that the earthly Jerusalem was no longer a holy city in the eyes of God the Father, nor any other place on the earth. Apostle Paul drives the point by comparing this earthly Jerusalem to the spiritual figure of Hagar, the slave of Sarah (**Galatians 4:25**). For Jesus, the worshipers His Father seeks – the spiritual sons of Sarah – are the ones who worship the Father in spirit and truth. Thus Jesus freed his Christians from the tyranny of holy places and days to which, alas for their misfortunes, the spiritual sons of Hagar – the inhabitants of the earthly Jerusalem – continue to submit.

Jesus has in fact freed Christians from all tyrannies, including that of holy meals. When asked about it, Apostle Paul answered:

> « *I know, and am persuaded by the Lord Jesus, that **there is nothing unclean of itself**: but to him that esteemeth any thing to be unclean, to him it is unclean*» (**Romans 14:14/ Bible 1769Authorized Version**).

> «*Therefore **let no one judge you in food or in drink, or in respect of a feast, or of the new moon, or of the sabbaths**. For these are a shadow of things to come, but the body is of Christ* (**Colossians 2:16-17**).

> «*If then you died with Christ from the elements of the world, **why, as though living in the world, are you subject to its ordinances: Touch not, taste not, handle not**; which things are all for corruption in the using, according to the commands and doctrines of men? These things indeed have a reputation of wisdom in self-imposed worship and humility, and unsparing severity of the body, **but are not of any value** for the satisfying of the flesh*» (**Colossians 2:20-23**).

The Christian is thus freed from the worship of holy days, holy places and holy meals.

Concretely, you can eat pork when people around consider it impure, while avoiding to provoke them – do it thus in private. You can eat beef in a world of vegetarians.

For the sake of the weak, however, he who esteems holy a day, a place or a meal, let him do it freely for God, without making others suffer, to avoid unnecessary conflicts.

The Lord knows that appearances are deceptive. What distinguishes a true Christian from a sorcerer disguised as a Christian? Nothing. Both can be confused. By getting rid of the tyranny of holy days, places and meals, the Lord is allowing us to live relaxed and free. He no longer wants caricatures of worshipers, mountain and caves worshipers. He wants worshipers in spirit and truth for His Father.

Free to learn everything

Have you not been barred from a professional career because you did not have the required diploma? Many have suffered this discrimination. A strong scientific knowledge is basically required for technical vocational training such as accountancy, computer science, medicine, aeronautics, etc.

Far from us to say that human systems of selection are not good. On the contrary, they are. What we want to point out is that the Lord is advising His children not to become discouraged if they do not have the requested diploma for a training course. It's all about learning a job. There are indeed strict certification programs. But there are many other opportunities to be trained without going through the traditional certification program. This is self-learning. May Christians feel free to learn what is worthy of interest.

Believe me, there are many training courses that do not require a certificate. Christians will have many choices. But still, if the Lord puts in the heart of the Christian to attend a training course, whether or not he has the required certificate, this Christian must thank the Lord and ask Him how to proceed. The Lord will show him the way. There are indeed many diploma equivalences. The Lord knows them all, even if the world ignores them or pretends to ignore them.

The Christian is free to take advantage of all the opportunities offered for training, whatever the field. Music is a field where many Christians exercise their talents without necessarily having the required diploma. Perhaps because in music matters, inspiration is more solicited than anything else; and inspiration is not dependent on the diploma. However if in music, one can progress without diploma, many other sectors can allow it. It will probably take more effort for the self-taught – it is not a certainty – but in the end, he will succeed.

That Christians feel free to learn everything according to their desire and availability. With the Lord Jesus Christ, everything is possible.

Conclusion

God intimately linked His children's journey to the ability of the windows of heaven to provide for themselves, rather than the resources of the earth. Neither Newton's laws, nor Einstein's laws, nor the prowess of electronics and the Internet websites, nor the quantum physics of the post-electronic age, can raise the dead, stop a storm or a tsunami, multiply bread, turn water into wine, heal the blind and various handicaps. These laws of science govern the earth. If God had intended to limit His Christians to the resources of the earth, there is no doubt that man, in his research, would have already reproduced the miracles of Christ mentioned in the Bible. The earth and its resources are simply too limited to offer Christians, solutions to their problems. Did God not tell Adam that the earth was cursed because of him, and that it would produce thorns and brambles as the result of his hard work? Can we imagine God asking His Christians to depend on such a cursed resource? Absurd.

When church leaders base their programs on the Christians' terrestrial revenues, following sharply fixed fee schedules, they give the impression of being good managers but, in the end, they offer a distressing spectacle that does not free them from rumors of mismanagement. Had Jesus not paid the Caesar's tax with the gold removed from Peter's hook, although the group He formed with the twelve disciples had a cashier? The existence of a membership fee does not prevent the Church from trusting and expecting the windows of heaven.

Glory to the Lord for having paved the way to the windows of heaven for His beloved children, because He loves and esteems them worthy to sit on His throne, as He Himself was worthy to sit on His Father's throne. Is it not wonderful that God gives His children heavenly Windows for their earthly needs? This is what Jesus did during His earthly journey which He punctuated with the excellent news that is:

> *«He who believes on Me (Jesus), **the works that I do he shall do also, and greater works than these he shall do**, because I go to My Father»* (**John 14:12**).

What are you waiting for dear Christians? Take advantage of these opportunities that the world does not know nor see. So that the world sees your works and glorifies the Heavenly Father.

Amen.

Table of contents

* 9 7 9 1 0 9 4 9 4 9 1 2 2 *